FRED WARD, BLACK STAR

*The 34th Annual Pictures of the Year Competition,
upon which this book is based, is supported by
an educational grant from Nikon, Inc.*

the best of PHOTOJOURNALISM 2

NEWSWEEK BOOKS, New York

National Press Photographers Association
University of Missouri School of Journalism

ALVIN GARFIN *Publisher*

Mary Ann Joulwan	*Art Director*
Edwin D. Bayrd, Jr.	*Editor*
Kathleen Berger	*Managing Editor*
Jared Lebow	*Contributing Editor*
Thomas Froncek	*Contributing Editor*

TITLE PAGE (left to right): William Yates, *Chicago Tribune* (Honorable mention, Spot News); top, Dale Atkins, *State News*, Michigan State University; bottom, Jim McTaggart, *The Minneapolis Star;* top, Larry Williams, *St. Louis Post-Dispatch;* bottom, David Rees, *San Bernardino Sun-Telegram;* top, Jay Mather, Denver Sentinel Newspapers; bottom, Michael S. Wirtz, *Suburban Trib,* Hinsdale, Illinois; top, Rich Frishman, Pioneer Press, Wilmette, Illinois; bottom, Robert Madden, *National Geographic;* George Thompson, *Suburban Trib,* Hinsdale, Illinois (Third place, Spot News).

Published in cooperation with the National Press Photographers Association, W.E. Garrett, Chairman, Book Committee; M. Jean Vile, Assistant.

Editorial matter, other textual material and compilation © 1977 by the National Press Photographers Association Foundation, Inc., Seattle, Washington.

For information concerning the Pictures of the Year Competition contact Charles Cooper, Executive Secretary of the National Press Photographers Association, Box 1146, Durham, North Carolina 27702

Library of Congress Cataloging in Publication Data
  National Press Photographers Association
  The Best of Photojournalism /2
  Index
1. Photography—Worldwide. 2. Photojournalism
3. 34th Annual Pictures of the Year Competition.
Library of Congress Card Number 77-081586
ISBN 0-88225-252-6

DAVID R. ATON, KETTERING-OAKWOOD TIMES

Contents

M ost of my working life has been spent in television news, where I have been intimately involved with pictures, the moving kind. But I retain an admiration for still photographs that I developed in my first year of working for a newspaper, many years ago. That paper was the *Minneapolis Times*, and unlike her two fatter competitors, she had few reporters. But she did have a number of staff photographers, whose work we used with a great deal of emphasis.

There is something about a big, clear black and white still. It does something that motion pictures can never do; it preserves a moment for eternity in a kind of half-tone amber. We in television news are justifiably proud of our coverage of the tragic days following the assassination of President Kennedy. But when you think back to those days, it is not the television pictures you remember. Television had film of Jack Ruby shooting Lee Harvey Oswald, and it was dramatic. In fact, television had plentiful coverage of all aspects of the Kennedy funeral. But the one picture you remember is a still taken by Robert H. Jackson, a black and white of young John-John saluting as his father's coffin passes by.

In television we have developed a number of special techniques for emphasizing certain images. Slow motion, for example. Was the receiver's foot in bounds when he caught the football? Look at the footage again, this time in slow motion. We also have what we call the "freeze frame," which means just that: stopping the moving picture to show a single frame. And what are these techniques—freeze frame and, to a lesser degree, slow motion—but a return to the still picture.

We do use still pictures in television, and perhaps we should use more of them and use them more effectively. I remember at least one occasion when a series of stills from the Associated Press led directly to an item's being included in a network news broadcast. The stills were Bob Scott's photos of young Teddy Kennedy, skiing for the first time after the amputation of his cancerous leg. I don't believe there was television film of this event; if so, I never saw it. It would have been interesting to see the motion, the actual skiing. But even a freeze frame from such a film would not, except accidentally, have had the composition of Scott's photos and would not, except accidentally, have captured the courage of a youngster determined to rise above a personal tragedy.

In a sense the motion photographer is like a dramatist, trying to record the action, the totality of an event. The still photographer is like a painter, always trying to compose that one perfect picture. In this book are 530 of those pictures, selected from among the 10,000 entries submitted to the thirty-fourth annual Pictures of the Year competition, which is conducted by the National Press Photographers Association and the University of Missouri School of Journalism and sponsored by an educational grant from Nikon, Inc. The title, *The Best of Photojournalism II*, involves a little poetic license, for "the best" is always a bit hard to determine. Judging photographs is a lot like judging what is news; there are no absolutes, and the determination is always subjective. You and I may have different ideas about whether one photograph is better than another, just as we have different ideas about whether a particular bit of information is news. So, if I cannot tell you that the photographs in this book are "the best," I can tell you that they are excellent, that they are among the best, and that they reflect the quality of the Pictures of the Year competition.

Shortly before the fall of Saigon, President Ford called the Vietnam War "a war that is finished," adding that "the time has come to look forward to an agenda for the future, to unify, to bind up the nation's wounds and to restore

Introduction

by Harry Reasoner

its health and its optimistic self-confidence." His listeners were college students, which was particularly appropriate, for it was students who had led the decade-long opposition to the war. For that decade Vietnam had preoccupied the nation and dominated her every act, ultimately dividing her people as nothing else had since the Civil War. The year 1976 did much "to unify, to bind up the nation's wounds." The war, it seemed, had been put behind us at last.

Helping to put the war behind us was our two-hundredth birthday party, a day of incredible good will and friendship. We were eager to play, to celebrate, to let happiness engulf us—and celebrate we did, all across the land. We went to rodeos in Nebraska. We played jazz in the streets of New Orleans. We rang church bells in Minnesota. We went to Independence Hall, to Valley Forge, to the Boston Commons to hear the Pops. We shot off fireworks. We picnicked. We paraded. We saw the Tall Ships sail majestically into New York harbor—a sight we had never seen before, nor will again. Kenneth Garrett's photograph on the back cover of this book recaptures that moment. Indeed, Garrett and several of his colleagues, represented in a special section of this book (pages 30–39), have preserved the Bicentennial for us. Television was there, of course, and its coverage was superb. As a matter of fact it can fairly be said that television helped foster the good will that marked our two-hundredth Fourth of July. But, again, it is the still photographs that we remember, the pictures imprinted on the mind.

The Bicentennial year was rife with patriotism, but there were instances of misplaced patriotism. Stanley J. Forman recorded one of those on pages 22–23—a graphic series of shots of antibusing demonstrators in Boston attacking a lone black man and ramming his head with a staff bearing the United States flag. Forman calls this series "The Soiling of Old Glory."

In 1976 we also elected a President. There were times, particularly during the worst days of Watergate, when many wondered whether our institutions would survive, whether we would ever again elect a President. But the center held, our "long national nightmare" ended, and the 1976 election campaign began in earnest. Jimmy Carter left his Georgia peanut farm to march through a seemingly endless succession of primaries. By the time he finished, people no longer asked, "Jimmy *who?*" And notwithstanding the *Milwaukee Sentinel* headline, held aloft a la Harry Truman by a grinning Carter on page 11, Mo Udall never beat Jimmy anywhere.

His primary victories gave Carter the Democratic presidential nomination before the convention even began. Ironically, it was the incumbent, President Ford, who had to fight for his party's nomination. The election campaign got under way with neither candidate surging clearly ahead—a closeness admirably reflected in Lawrence Frank's striking double-image photo (page 9) of the last of the presidential debates. (Incidentally, an estimated 90 million Americans watched those televised debates. That's roughly 10 million more than actually voted.) In the closeness of the popular vote, which gave Carter a lead of just 1,680,940 votes out of 80 million cast, the people told Gerald Ford that they approved of his caretaker presidency—and they told Jimmy Carter that they wanted a new man in the White House.

In 1976, we had 3 million births—and 2 million deaths. We had 2 million marriages—and 1 million divorces. We also had our share of disasters, natural and man made. The Teton Dam in Idaho burst, killing nine and forcing 30,000 from their homes. Flash floods roared through Colorado's Big Thompson Canyon, taking another 139 lives. Giulio Broglio covered a major earthquake in eastern Turkey, distilling the suffering there into one heart-wrenching shot (pages 52–53) of a small boy digging in the rubble for his mother. And William Garrett and Robert Madden took their cameras to Guatemala to record—on the front cover and on pages 46–49—the aftermath of the worst earthquake in Central American history.

The year had its sports highlights too. Some thirty nations, mostly African, boycotted the summer Olympic Games in Montreal for political reasons, but that did not detract from Bruce Jenner's record-setting victory in the decathlon. Nor did it take anything away from the stunning performance of Romania's fourteen-year-old wonder, Nadia Comaneci, whose perfect score in gymnastics was the first ever in the Olympics. The year also had some low moments in sports. J. D. Patrick recorded one of them with two stills entitled "Hockey?" (pages 238–39).

In 1976 the mysterious "Legionnaire's disease" claimed the lives of 28 persons who attended a convention in Philadelphia. Shortly thereafter federal health authorities warned of a possible epidemic of swine flu and inaugurated a nationwide program of inoculations. This gave Christopher Stewart his wry feature shot (page 24) of a survivor of the 1918 flu epidemic getting his swine flu injection. (Stewart took his picture in California, but that wonderful face could have come from my boyhood Iowa.)

In 1976 Howard Hughes, a man not noted for friendliness toward photographers, died. And the New Jersey Supreme Court ruled that Karen Anne Quinlan had the right to die. Doctors disconnected her life-support equipment, but she lived on. In 1976 private citizens Richard and Pat Nixon visited China, a month and a half after Chou En-lai's death and seven months before Mao Tse-tung's. In 1976 airborne Israeli commandos electrified the world with a daring raid on Uganda's Entebbe airport that freed 103 hostages from pro-Palestine guerrillas. Also in 1976: Concorde SST flights began—to Washington, but not New York; Wayne Hays ran afoul of Elizabeth Ray; and Patty Hearst was convicted of armed robbery. We had our customary share of violent crimes in 1976: some 19,000 murders, 400,000 robberies, 55,000 rapes. The numbers are both impressive and frightening.

In short, the year was the usual mixed bag of good and bad, of the whole range of the human experience. And the still photographer was on hand to record it. The *Wall Street Journal*, which does not use photos itself, nevertheless took note of the rising market for photographs in a long feature story. The paper quoted Weston Naef, an associate curator of the Metropolitan Museum of Art, as saying, "It's been a long time coming, but the general public now is realizing the enormous difficulty of making a really great photograph—that not just anybody who uses a camera is an artist."

The photographers within these pages are artists, and the value of their work can be measured in dollars; this year a single photograph by Charles Sheeler brought $8,750 at an auction in New York City.

Another example of the value we place on photographs is Canada's Bicentennial gift to the United States, a handsome volume of 220 pictures taken along both sides of our common, unguarded 5,200-mile border. In the pages of *Photojournalism/76*, this book's predecessor, Howard Chapnick, president of the photographic agency Black Star, argued for publishing not a collector's item book, such as Canada's Bicentennial gift, but a quality soft-cover photographic book at a popular price. "The opportunities in photographic book publishing are there," Chapnick said.

While he did not specifically address his words to the National Press Photographers Association or to Newsweek Books, they must have heard him, for here is the book Chapnick wanted: *The Best of Photojournalism II*.

National News

LAWRENCE FRANK, THE DAILY IOWAN

A hundred years from now 1976 will be remembered, before all else, as the year the United States celebrated its two-hundredth birthday. Those who plan the nation's Tricentennial will naturally wish to know how we handled our Bicentennial festivities, and their research may well lead them to this volume. An optimistic thought, perhaps, but then 1976 was an optimistic year. You will find no shots of American soldiers burning Southeast Asian villages in this book, nor will you find pictures of a corrupt President resigning his office. What you will find are photographs of a new President, elected by a resilient political system that had weathered Watergate. The 1976 national election produced the first series of presidential debates since 1960—the subject of Lawrence Frank's unique double exposure above. And although the most exciting moments were the twenty minutes of silence induced by technical difficulties, the debates did give us an opportunity to study the men who sought to lead us as they acted and reacted under pressure. Even in a year dominated by good news there was some of the bad to photograph and document. Here, as elsewhere, racial discord remained a potent threat to social stability and civic order, particularly in the nation's largest cities. In Boston, for example, savage street brawling followed a federal judge's insistence that a controversial busing program be put into effect. And while blood was being spilled in the streets of Boston, some 7.5 million gallons of oil were being spilled off the coast of nearby Nantucket Island as the tanker *Argo Merchant* split in half. What else happened in 1976? Remember swine flu, amnesty for draft resistors, and the passing of Chicago's long-time mayor, Richard J. Daley? These and other major news events of the Bicentennial year are recalled in the photographs that are included in this section under the general heading of National News.

DENNIS BRACK, BLACK STAR (HONORABLE MENTION, CAMPAIGN '76/MAG)

LLOYD MOEBIUS, FLINT JOURNAL (SECOND PLACE, CAMPAIGN '76)

Campaign '76 began with a series of presidential primaries that saw Ronald Reagan off to a flying start (top, left) in his two-man race with President Gerald Ford for the Republican nomination, while a former Georgia peanut farmer— dubbed "Jimmy who?" by some skeptics—surprised virtually everyone by getting a quick jump (top, right) on the large field of Democratic hopefuls. The premature headline opposite— Udall actually lost Wisconsin— gave Jimmy Carter one of many opportunities to flash his toothy grin, soon to become the world's most famous smile.

Vice President Nelson Rockefeller was nothing if not irrepressible— as he was to demonstrate at the Republican Convention in Kansas City after an irate Reaganite ripped out the telephone connecting Rocky's New York delegation with the podium.

There are times in every campaign that try men's souls, not to mention their patience and tempers. Most veteran politicians choose to counter the insults hurled at them by hostile audiences in one of two ways: by simply ignoring the heckler's taunts or by tossing back a witty—and often well-rehearsed —rejoinder. Such was not the case when Vice President Nelson Rockefeller addressed a crowd of rowdy students in Binghamton, New York. Faced with a classic obscenity, he returned the salute in kind—a gesture that Don Black recorded for posterity in this prize-winning photograph.

LAWRENCE FRANK, THE DAILY IOWAN

Every convention has one winner and many losers. Here are but two: a man who backed the losing Republican candidate; and Elizabeth Ray, who won national attention when she revealed her affair with Congressman Wayne Hays but lost her own bid to gain admittance to the convention as a magazine correspondent.

Obviously a Ford supporter, this woman represents a tiny minority group within a large minority group. According to the Joint Center for Political Studies, which analyzed black voting patterns, an estimated two-thirds of all registered blacks voted, and roughly 94 percent of them cast their ballots for the Democratic ticket. These votes proved decisive in closely contested states like Louisiana, New York, Ohio, Pennsylvania, and Texas. The results left Republican strategists dismayed over how to attract these voters back to the party of Lincoln before 1980.

EDDIE ADAMS, ASSOCIATED PRESS

Election Day dawned sunny and dry as 55 percent of all those Americans eligible to vote made their way to the polls. Everyone had predicted a close race and that is exactly how things turned out. Not until the early hours of the morning after did it become apparent that Gerald Ford was going to become the first chief executive since Herbert Hoover to be voted out of office—and that Jimmy Carter would be the first President elected from the Deep South since before the Civil War. The final count showed Carter with a 51-48 majority of the popular vote. It had not been easy, but "Jimmy who?" had made the transition from Georgia peanut farmer to President.

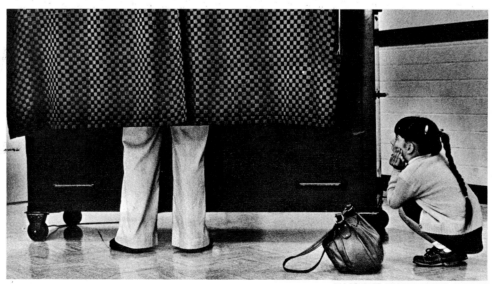

17

The long campaign is over, but the memories linger on. Among the images that will not fade is this picture of Robert Dole, taken the day he was chosen the Republican vice presidential candidate. Speaking before an audience of hometown friends in Russell, Kansas, Dole began to weep as he recalled their efforts in helping him recover from the wounds he suffered in World War II. (Dole had lost the use of three limbs and his chances for recovery seemed slight until his friends banded together to raise money for his rehabilitation.) But for all the public moments there are also times of the most intense privacy. A candidate—even if he is the President, as Gerald Ford was when Bob Brown caught him in silhouette at right—often finds himself waiting for the signal to step back into the spotlight.

*Throughout his twenty-one years
as mayor of Chicago—a term
without precedent in the Windy
City's history—Richard J. Daley
occupied this chair during City
Council meetings. His death in
December of 1976 at the age of
seventy-four left a large void in
Midwestern American politics,
one that will not soon be filled.*

Boston, cradle of the Revolution, was witness to intense racial discord during the Bicentennial year. Strong opposition to a court-ordered busing plan for the public school system provided the catalyst for violent encounters such as this one, which occurred near City Hall. It began when a black businessman named Theodore Landsmark walked through Government Center shortly after the break-up of an antibusing demonstration. A gang of young white toughs, having just completed the Pledge of Allegiance, used the flagstaff to spear Landsmark (left) and then punched and kicked at the defenseless man (above) until police finally rescued him from his attackers and placed four of them under arrest. Boston Herald American photographer Stanley Forman won a Pulitzer Prize for his coverage of this incident, the second consecutive year that Forman has been so honored.

STANLEY FORMAN, BOSTON HERALD AMERICAN (FIRST PLACE, SPOT NEWS)

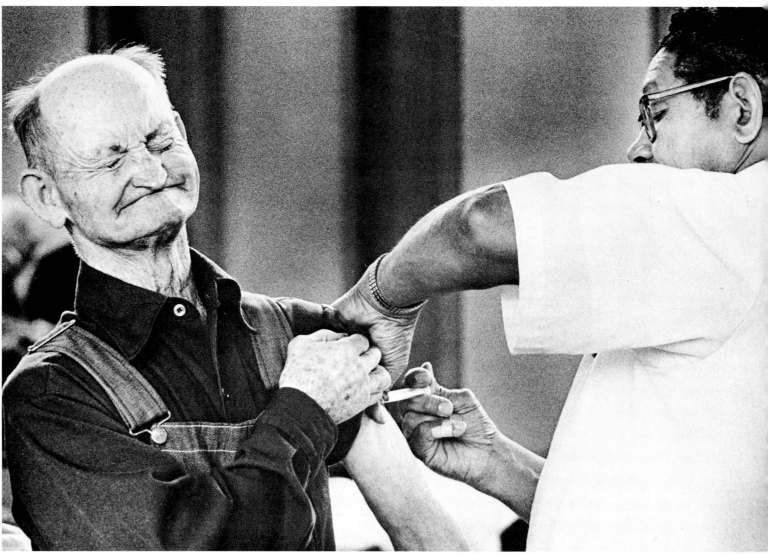

CHRISTOPHER STEWART, WATSONVILLE REGISTER-PAJARONIAN

Remember the swine flu epidemic of 1976? Congress appropriated some $135 million to immunize Americans against this dreaded strain of influenza virus—and the Department of Health, Education and Welfare suspended the program after only two months because 517 people came down with a serious neurological disorder after getting their shots. Twenty-three of those people died. Total number of swine flu cases reported: six. One of those to receive a shot—and survive— was Temple Starkey (above), who also survived the great influenza epidemic of 1918.

His presidency was not six hours old when Jimmy Carter fulfilled a campaign promise by pardoning Vietnam draft resistors. His move was intended to heal over the divisiveness caused by the war, but for a time it only stirred fresh controversy. Numerous veterans' organizations expressed dismay (above), and Senator Barry Goldwater called it "the most disgraceful thing a President has ever done." The pardon covered 13,000 men who had avoided the draft and 250,000 who had failed to register for it. It did not effect the 100,000 men who entered the armed forces and later deserted.

A week after it ran aground on sandy shoals off Massachusetts' Nantucket Island, the Argo Merchant, a Liberian-flag oil tanker, split apart and spilled 7.5 million gallons of heavy oil into the sea. Environmental Protection Agency administrator Russell Train called the disaster the "nation's biggest oil spill." The pollution threatened both the rich Georges Bank fishing area and the beaches of nearby Cape Cod.

OVERLEAF: Only minutes after a capacity crowd filed out of Baltimore's Memorial Stadium following a National Football League playoff game between the Pittsburgh Steelers and the Baltimore Colts, this light plane crashed into the stadium's upper deck. Miraculously, the pilot suffered only minor injuries and none of the spectators were hurt. P.S. Pittsburgh won.

BRYAN MOSS, LOUISVILLE COURIER-JOURNAL

RICHARD HORWITZ, ASSOCIATED PRESS

The men on page 30 were there when it all began. Alexander Milliner (top), Daniel Waldo (bottom), and William Hutchings all served in Washington's revolutionary army and were the last survivors of the fighting force that made possible our recent Bicentennial celebrations. These ranged from the ridiculous—such as the demonstration at right of how not to fire an old flintlock musket—to the sublime beauty of Operation Sail. The July Fourth holiday extended from Mars Hill, Maine, where dawn's early light struck the continental United States at 4:31 A.M., to a point 200 million miles into space, where, a few hours later, America's Viking I lander slid quietly through the vapor-thin atmosphere of Mars to settle softly on the mysterious Red Planet's sandy surface. In Philadelphia, the Queen of England presented that city with a six-ton commemorative bell. In Washington, President Ford witnessed a $200,000 fireworks display, while in Boston Arthur Fiedler conducted before an outdoor audience of some 200,000 people. All in all, it was a joyous birthday party for the world's most durable democracy.

For all their glitter, none of the other Bicentennial spectacles matched the gathering of 225 sailing ships from thirty nations that cruised up and down New York's Hudson River during Operation Sail. The thousands of people who crowded onto apartment-house terraces (right) formed only a small part of the crowd, estimated in the millions, that packed both sides of the river for glimpses of majestic vessels like Denmark's Christian Danmark, *photographed above through the twin towers of the World Trade Center. Built in 1932, this 253-foot-long vessel was visiting New York's 1939 World's Fair when World War II broke out. She stayed for the duration of the war, serving as a training ship for some 5,000 Coast Guard cadets.*

The 298-foot-long Portuguese bark Sagres II, built in 1937, sails down the Hudson River with the George Washington Bridge in the background. This photograph was taken from the afterdeck of Dar Pomorza, a 299-foot-long Polish ship that was built in 1909. In all, some sixteen "Tall Ships" took part in the naval review. Two of them represented the United States: the Gazelia Primero, a 187-foot barkentine built in 1883; and Eagle, a 295-foot bark built in 1936 and now used as a Coast Guard training vessel. The smaller craft shown here, those with yellow and black spinnakers, are U.S. Naval Academy yawls.

OPPOSITE: KEN REGAN, CAMERA 5, NEWSWEEK; ABOVE: KIT LUCE

Every American has a dual heritage, for only pure-blooded Indians are true native Americans. The rest, including those who trace their heritage back to the country's Founding Fathers, are émigrés. And on July 4, 1976, all had reason to celebrate their U.S. citizenship. In Boston an Armenian businessman donated $25,000 for a municipal fireworks display, and in New Jersey a patriotic homeowner painted his clapboard siding red, white, and blue (above). The scale differed, but the sentiment was the same. The rockets' red glare was visible across the land, but nowhere did it glow more brightly than over the Statue of Liberty (opposite).

And everywhere there were flags.
Fluttering in serried ranks on
either side of Chestnut Street in
downtown Philadelphia (above),
where the Declaration of
Independence was signed two
hundred years earlier. And high
above Veterans' Stadium—also in
Philadelphia—where agile Karl
Wallenda, senior member of the
famed high-wire act, unfurled
both the Stars and Stripes and the
Bicentennial flag (right) during a
between-games exhibition.

The parades had all passed by, the bunting had come down, and it was time to take in the flags, purchased in a national flush of reborn patriotism. Alan Berner's evocative photograph catches two members of a Fulton, Missouri, Boy Scout troop struggling to stack the flags they had carried in a Lincoln Day procession.

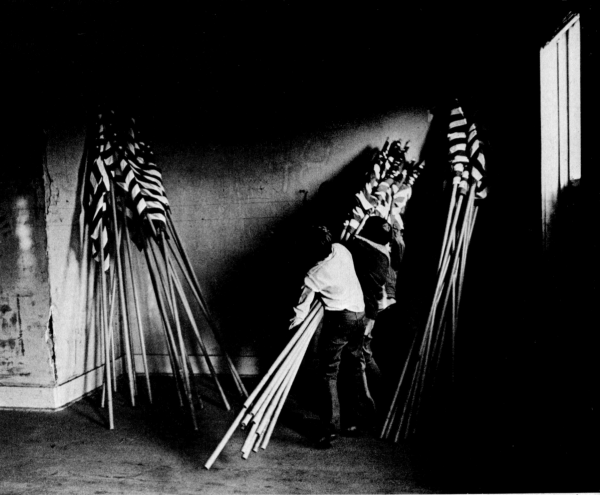

CHUCK MCGOWEN, WILMINGTON NEWS-JOURNAL

ALAN BERNER, COLUMBIA DAILY TRIBUNE (SECOND PLACE, PICTORIAL)

GENE PUSKAR

International News

In the most superficial sense, 1976 was a tranquil year, free of large-scale conflict in both Southeast Asia and the Middle East. But President Ford's election-trail claim that the world was at peace for the first time in a generation had a singularly hollow ring in many corners of the world. In Lebanon, for example, opposing factions were to reduce Beirut, one of the legendary cities of the Levant, to rubble. And powerful seismic disturbances were to produce even greater rubble heaps—and claim thousands of lives—in Central America and eastern Turkey, in Gemona, Italy, and Tangshan, China. Governments fell in Argentina and Thailand, and the burgeoning Lockheed scandal threatened others in Japan and the Netherlands. No single continent dominated the international news in 1976, but one—Africa—came close. From Angola to Rhodesia, from the Union of South Africa to Ethiopia, the Dark Continent was in a state of almost constant political ferment. And nowhere was the struggle more bitter— or the human toll higher—than in the all-black township of Soweto, an urban hellhole some twenty miles outside Johannesburg, South Africa. Soweto, which has but two cinemas and thirty-five public telephones for its estimated population of 1.3 million, also has a crime rate unequaled by any major city on earth. To get to the mines and factories of Johannesburg, where most of the residents of Soweto work, nonwhites must carry a government-issued passbook (above) and obey strictly enforced curfews. Violaters are often detained indefinitely by the police, and a suspiciously high number of dissidents die while in custody. Rebelling against these and other abridgments of their rights, blacks rioted in the streets of Soweto in June. When peace was finally restored, 140 lay dead, two of them white, and 1,128 had been injured, six of them white. In addition, police had jailed 894 others—all of whom were black.

One fifth of all the urban blacks in Africa live in Soweto, whose regimented rows of flimsy, government-built housing are half-hidden, in the photograph opposite, by the shifting haze from thousands of cookstoves. More stockade than metropolis, Soweto boasts none of the expected urban amenities, and its dusty streets are overrun by tsotsis, vicious local gangsters who prey upon hapless workers whose pay averages a paltry $21 per month. Soweto and cities like it are a direct outgrowth of an ambitious segregation program undertaken by the white minority government of South Africa as a means of consolidating and perpetuating its hold over a population that is 82 percent nonwhite. To achieve this goal the present government has systematically relocated millions of blacks. Above: uprooted members of the Bakalobeng tribe are transported to the new town of Deelpan. Below: temporary housing for displaced Zulus.

JAMES P. BLAIR, NATIONAL GEOGRAPHIC (SECOND PLACE, DOCUMENTARY PICTURE STORY)

To the "white tribe" that rules South Africa, apartheid means the separation of the races; to black tribesmen it more often means dislocation, disease, and death. During the past eight years, for instance, 900 children have died of malnutrition and related illnesses in Dimbaza, a new resettlement village not far from Port Elizabeth on the southeast coast. Headstones are a luxury the citizens of Dimbaza can ill afford, so these little graves are marked by stakes, each surmounted by a fading number. Many, the tiny gravesite above among them, are personalized by the addition of a somewhat ironic totem—the dead child's white-skinned doll. It is small comfort to the women (left) who buried these children that the village of Dimbaza now has water and their men have some means of earning a modest living.

W. E. GARRETT, NATIONAL GEOGRAPHIC

The severe earthquake that struck central Guatemala at 3:02 A.M. on February 4, 1976, quite literally tore the country in two. The initial shock lasted only half a minute, but it hit with ninety times the force of the quake that had razed Managua, Nicaragua, four years earlier. It split the small Central American nation from ocean to ocean, leaving 23,000 dead in its wake. Another 77,000 were injured, either in the main quake or during six days of aftershocks, and a million people were left homeless. Small villages like El Progresso, above, which lay along the east-west line known as the Motagua Fault, were leveled instantly; rescue teams found only three buildings still standing when they reached El Progresso, which is not far from Gualán, the epicenter of the quake. One rescuer reported: "As we entered the town, one man was screaming in the ruins. 'He has just found the bodies of both his parents,' a volunteer explained. The man was still screaming when neighbors took him away." With food, water, and medicine in short supply, queues (right) formed wherever provisions were available.

ROBERT W. MADDEN, NATIONAL GEOGRAPHIC

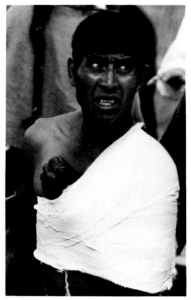

ABOVE, W.E. GARRETT; ALL OTHERS, ROBERT W. MADDEN

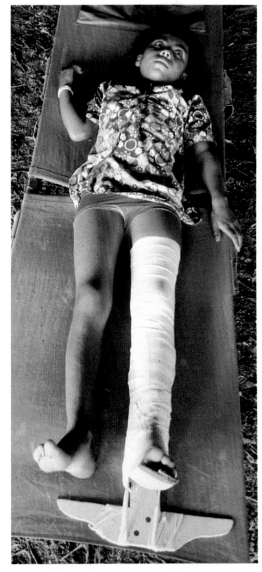

At Zacapa, not fifty miles from the quake's center, the injured were treated outdoors (above) for fear that the weakened hospital might collapse during one of the many successive aftershocks. U.S. Army doctors, flown in to assist local medical men, dubbed their tent-hospital "Central Casting" in honor of all the limbs they set with makeshift splints (left). While medics tended the hurt, those who were unhurt masked themselves against the stench of bodies being cremated (left, below) and sifted through the ruins. For many—the woman opposite, for one— there was precious little to recover. For others, among them a woman from Zacapa who had been mute for more than a year, there was more. Her powers of speech miraculously restored, the old woman exclaimed, "Great power of God! My children!"

A human skull, hoisted by the smiling children at left, seems an apt symbol for the civil war that tore Lebanon apart and left the city of Beirut in ruins. Death was the only real victor in this bitter fratricidal conflict between Christians and Moslems; of more than 20,000 Lebanese killed, the bulk were innocent civilians. Prisoners were rarely taken on either side, captives were often summarily executed on the basis of religious affiliation alone, and corpses were frequently badly mutilated. Hopes for peace were dashed again and again as new ceasefire agreements were reached—only to be shattered by a new outburst of fighting. In the long fighting, barely two square miles of Beirut real estate changed hands, but as the war went on the weapons employed became more and more lethal—until even surface-to-surface missiles were being used and once-safe residential sections were being shelled by both sides. Lebanon became a country with no police force, no army, and no effective government. Gunmen ruled the streets, and for people like the Christian woman below and the Moslem woman at right, all that remained was prayer and fear.

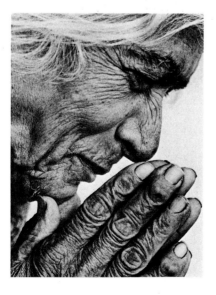

In 1976 more people were killed by earthquakes than in any year since 1927. Quakes were not unusually numerous, but many of them hit densely populated areas—Guatemala City, the southern Philippines, and Hopei Province in China, where, by most foreign estimates, at least 100,000 people died. In late November the earth shook in eastern Turkey, in the area between Lake Van and Mount Ararat, where the Bible says Noah's ark came to rest. In the town of Caldarin, half the population of 2,500 was killed. Giulio Broglio was there to photograph the destruction, and his take included this poignant shot of a small boy digging in the rubble for his mother.

Thailand's "Monument to Democracy" stands a half mile from the gates of Thammasat University in Bangkok. By the time the Vietnam War ended, Thailand had endured more than twenty years of military rule, and the Thais would joke that the monument had been named, "because that's where they've got democracy locked up." In October, after a three-year experiment with parliamentary government, Thailand's military used the pretext of a bloody riot to lock democracy up again. Photographer Neal Ulevich recorded the unrestrained savagery that occurred when right-wing groups, backed by 1,500 heavily armed police, attacked leftist students.

NEAL ULEVICH, ASSOCIATED PRESS (FIRST PLACE, NEWS PICTURE STORY)

Before the bloodbath ended, thirty-nine students had been beaten to death, beheaded, or hanged. Even death provided no escape for some of the victims, as these grisly photographs indicate. Rightists hung corpses from trees and pounded them with clubs and chairs, then cut them down, doused them with gasoline, and gleefully set them on fire. Luckier students were herded into an athletic field, stripped to the waist, and forced to crawl between rows of policemen who clubbed them and tore small images of the Buddha from around their necks—"because Communists are not Buddhists." The 1976 coup was Thailand's fourteenth since World War II.

NEAL ULEVICH, ASSOCIATED PRESS (SECOND PLACE, SPOT NEWS)

People

It was an all too familiar story for a magazine photographer: the magnificent cover shot that never appeared on the cover. Photographer Eddie Adams, assigned to do a series of portraits of Diana Ross for the cover of *Time* magazine, set the studio scene carefully. He had the singer dress in the exotic costumes she was wearing in her current New York show and he played her albums in the background to create a show mood. The combination clicked. The resulting portrait, reproduced here, shows a befeathered Diana Ross who is as sleek as a cat and as fanciful as a character out of Dr. Seuss. A sure cover? Sure . . . except that the editors decided to feature another important personality that particular week. A similar fate befell Murry Sill's shot of Lester Maddox strong-arming a potential voter; Sill's editors chose a more flattering shot of the ex-governor instead. Happily, the original images survive. They are joined in this portfolio by revealing portraits of a variety of other personalities, famous, infamous, and ordinary, some of them posed and some snapped on the run. They include: Salvatore DiMarco's shot of piano virtuoso Arthur Rubinstein performing in Philadelphia at the age of eighty-nine; Dan Farrell's candid glimpse of straphanger Bing Crosby on his way to the race track; Harry Benson's shot of author Truman Capote hamming it up for the readers of *People* magazine; Wally McNamee's impression of citizen Richard Nixon basking in the applause of a group of Chinese schoolchildren; Bob Aylott's look into the eyes of Charles Manson, mastermind of the Tate-LaBianca murders; David Roese's portrait of Grandpa Goddard, self-styled sex counselor of Lakemore, Ohio; Earl Morris's startling photo of an armed robber, caught at the instant he shoots himself to death; and Philip Gould's prize-winning photograph of mourners at the funeral of guitarist Mance Lipscomb.

Richard Nixon was photographed by Wally McNamee during the former President's trip to China in February, 1976. The trip marked Nixon's first public appearance following his resignation, and McNamee was one of twenty journalists the Chinese allowed to cover the event. Fred Ward shot his portrait of Fidel Castro while doing an essay on Cuba. "Early in my visit," wrote Ward, "I had requested an interview with . . . Castro. As is his style, no acknowledgment was made. Two days before my departure I suddenly got a call that he would pick me up at the hotel's front door in seven minutes. Cameras were all over the room, my tape recorder packed . . . and I needed to shower and shave. But how could I keep him waiting? When I neared the lobby door, out of breath, I could see the large, familiar figure in green fatigues sitting in the front seat of an open Soviet-made jeep guarded by armed soldiers." The informal portrait of Helmut Schmidt and Willy Brandt below was taken just prior to West Germany's national elections, during a campaign luncheon for prominent politicians held in the Rathskeller of Munich's City Hall.

FRED WARD, BLACK STAR

ROBERT W. MADDEN, NATIONAL GEOGRAPHIC

SUZANNE VLAMIS, ASSOCIATED PRESS

"He's easy to photograph," says Harry Benson of noted author Truman Capote, subject of the portrait on the opposite page. "He's an old clown. He'll pose for anything." Benson shot this picture at the writer's apartment in New York City, and it appeared as part of a cover story on Capote that ran in People magazine. In the portrait above, Suzanne Vlamis has caught John F. Kennedy, Jr. and his sister Caroline exchanging a few words as they watch the Robert F. Kennedy Celebrity Tennis Tournament at Forest Hills, New York. The children of the late President and Jacqueline Kennedy Onassis were among those who turned out in August of 1976 to watch luminaries from the worlds of politics, sports, and show business compete in a charity event that raises funds for the Robert F. Kennedy Memorial.

Arthur Rubinstein (above) was photographed at age eighty-nine at the Philadelphia Academy of Music in March, 1976, when he appeared in a special anniversary concert with the Philadelphia Orchestra. Rubinstein had first played in America seventy years earlier, also with the Philadelphia Orchestra. Bing Crosby was discovered in rather less elegant surroundings—a New York City subway car (right). The famous singer was on his way to Aqueduct Race Track.

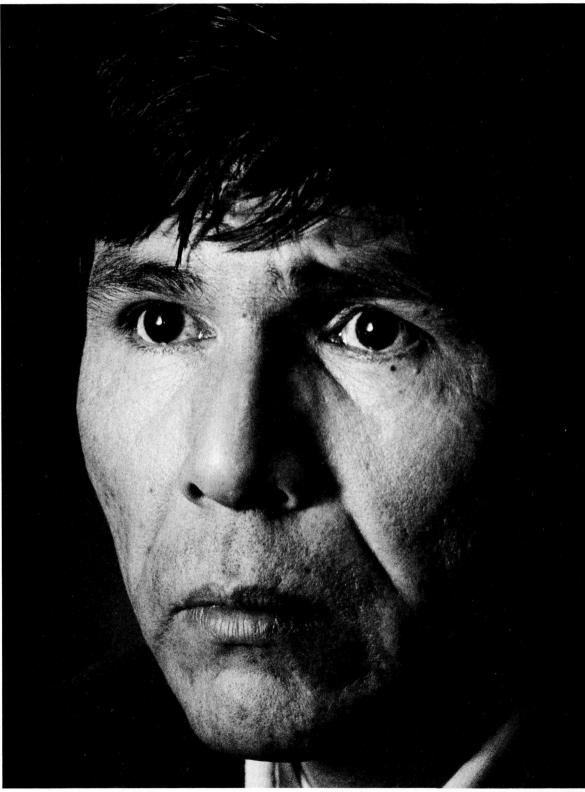

STEPHANIE MAZE, SAN FRANCISCO CHRONICLE

The three men whose portraits appear on these pages share a common bond: each is a man with a cause. Dennis Banks (opposite), the leader of the American Indian Movement, was in California facing extradition to South Dakota when he was photographed. Banks had been convicted of riot and assault during the Wounded Knee occupation of the Pine Ridge reservation in 1972. He had gone underground prior to his court conviction but later turned up in California, where he became the center of a campaign aimed at persuading Governor Brown not to extradite him. Given the political climate in South Dakota, argued Banks's defenders,

extradition would be tantamount to a death sentence. The case is still under appeal. Arguing another case—"the insanity of nuclear retaliation"—was Philip Berrigan (above), former priest and self-styled "cornerstone of the resistance to the war in Indochina." Berrigan was photographed during a reception at a Unitarian church in Fort Lauderdale, Florida. Attorney William Kunstler (right) headed the defense team in the trial of Darrelle Butler and Robert Robideau, accused of taking part in the fatal shooting of two FBI agents during the Wounded Knee occupation. Kunstler had also defended Daniel Berrigan and Dennis Banks, among others.

Awaiting the verdict in their retrial in connection with a 1966 murder case, the ex-prize fighter Rubin "Hurricane" Carter and John Artis pose in the doorway of the Hudson County, New Jersey, courthouse. In 1967 the men, found guilty of shooting down three people in a Paterson bar, had been sentenced to life terms in prison. A retrial was ordered early in 1976 after two key witnesses recanted their sworn testimony. In the retrial, Carter and Artis were again found guilty, but that decision, too, is under appeal. No such legal doubts surround the case of Charles Manson (opposite), the "messiah of murder" who is serving eight consecutive life terms for having masterminded the Tate-LaBianca killings of 1969. Photographed during an interview held in the psychiatric unit of the California Medical Facility at Vacaville, Manson was quoted as saying: "It didn't matter who was killed as long as it was someone. No one was picked—no one picked out Sharon Tate . . . I wasn't there in the house that night, but I was there in spirit."

"The Boxer," left, slit-eyed and battle-scarred, was discovered panhandling in the vicinity of an Indianapolis bus terminal. He told Bob Dickerson that he was trying to get enough money together to catch a bus to Louisville, where he had a boxing engagement lined up for the following night. "He was a spooky character," recalls Dickerson. "He asked me if I would give him some money. I asked him if I could take his picture. I got the picture and he got some money." Bryan Grigsby was on assignment for his paper, covering a tobacco auction near High Springs, Florida, when he shot the photo on the opposite page. The subject, a short-term inmate of a nearby prison, was being paid to load bales of tobacco amid the dust and heat of a tobacco warehouse.

Blues guitarist Mance Lipscomb came from the soil, and when he returned to the earth last year his numerous colleagues and comrades turned out to say farewell. Like Mance, many of them were black, and many were old—farmers and friends, field hands and fellow musicians. Philip Gould found these four lingering outside the church in Navasota, Texas, where the Lipscomb funeral was held.

PHILIP GOULD, DALLAS TIMES HERALD (FIRST PLACE, PICTORIAL)

MURRY SILL, AIKEN STANDARD

In the photo at left, Murry Sill captures something of Lester Maddox's aggressive campaign style—and one voter's reaction. Maddox was campaigning for President in Aiken, South Carolina, a week before the 1976 election. The open-handed approach of Albert Gore, Jr. (opposite) was not much more successful, at least on this foray into the hustings during his campaign for Congress in a predominantly rural district of Tennessee. Gore, who is the son of the long-time senator from Tennessee, eventually caught up with this prospective constituent and won a handshake. He also won a seat in Congress.

NANCY WARNECKE, NASHVILLE TENNESSEAN (FIRST PLACE, CAMPAIGN '76)

RICH FRISHMAN, PIONEER PRESS

When the Record of Lawrence County, Missouri, was looking for local subjects for its regular human interest feature, "Faces," photographer Rebecca Collette knew just which faces to go after: those of Donnie and Ronnie Wright (below), who are the twin policemen of Mount Vernon, Missouri. When appropriate, the Wright brothers switch hats and uniforms and serve as firemen. Hats are only one facet of the business run by "Panama Joe," above, in his novelty store, The Schlock Shop.

REBECCA COLLETTE, LAWRENCE COUNTY RECORD

BRUCE BISPING, MINNEAPOLIS TRIBUNE

BOB MODERSOHN, DES MOINES REGISTER

A workman repairing a fountain in Minneapolis becomes part of the sculpture in the Bruce Bisping photograph above. The subject of the portrait at left is Roy "Snake" White, who once played trumpet with such jazz greats as Louis Armstrong, Count Basie, and Fletcher Henderson. He has since retired to Iowa, where Bob Modersohn photographed him in his backyard woodshed. The notes on the wall behind him mark the heights he was able to hit before being fitted with "these Sears Roebuck teeth."

Holiday or not, July 4, 1976 was a workday for John Monnahan, 82 (standing, at left), and his brother Walter, 64, who still farm the land in eastern Colorado that their parents homesteaded in 1909 and who still live in the family's original four-room sod house. They are survivors. Their parents have died, their brothers and sisters have moved away. The two have experienced depression, recession, inflation, drought, and flood. But they continue to live by the rhythms of the land, the weather, and the seasons. Even on holidays there are fences to mend, cows to be milked, fields to be plowed. The big farming operations, with plenty of extra hands and thousands of acres, can pause for breath now and then; if one crop fails there are others to help make up for the loss. The Monnahans have to manage pretty much on their own, relying on one or two crops to get them through. "We might lose it all in one hailstorm," says Walter. That they have made it this long is a tribute to their perseverance and fortitude.

JAY MATHER, DENVER SENTINEL NEWSPAPERS

Negotiations (above) on a new
three-year contract between the
United Auto Workers and General
Motors began on an ebullient
note with a cordial handshake
between the U.A.W.'s Leonard
Woodcock, at left, and George
Morris, vice president in charge of
labor relations at G.M. No such
enthusiasm was apparent among
the Virginia lawmakers opposite,
who were caught napping toward
the end of a twenty-five-hour
legislative session.

BOB BROWN, RICHMOND NEWSPAPERS

Rich Frishman has been taking photographs of the denizens of Chicago's Madison Street skid row for nine years. "I wanted to see another side of life," he says. The result has been a series of striking photographs and long tape-recorded interviews. The portrait above, taken during the summer of 1976, is of Clinton Fields, who told Frishman: "Last place I lived they tore down. Somebody stole my Bible, too. . . . I can't get my welfare money cause I don't have no birth record. I don't have no birth record cause my Mama and Daddy wasn't married. . . . Sometimes I think I'm dead. Sometimes I think I'm dead and living in hell." The man opposite, below, had little to say, but "Jim," far right, waxed metaphorical: "This is skid row: a bunch of broken stinkin' teeth. You wanna come down here to show the world what life is like on skid row and you can't even stand to look at it. I got it in my hands and you can't even stand to look at it."

OVERLEAF: *The fare is hardly Lucullan, and the ambience is early alleyway, but neither fact has diminished the appetite of Jack Boyd, a sixty-two-year-old Texan who has assembled a feast for himself from the garbage cans behind a Miami restaurant.*

MICHAEL O'BRIEN, MIAMI NEWS

RICH FRISHMAN, PIONEER PRESS

"I can't surrender," were the words of the desperate gunman opposite, who shot himself to death before a horrified group of St. Louis newsmen and police in July, 1976. Earl Morris snapped the shutter at the instant Gregory Moore pulled the trigger. Moore had been holding four tavern customers hostage after being cornered by police during an armed robbery. Police officers and clergymen spent three hours trying to talk Moore into releasing his hostages and laying down his gun. When at last he came to the door with one of the hostages it seemed he was about to give up. But as television cameramen and photographers pressed closer, Moore said: "I can't surrender. I got a case pending against me. No, I got two cases. I'll do it right now." Then he cocked his pistol and shot himself through the right temple. At left: An anonymous prison inmate's eye, reflected in a piece of broken mirror.

87

When Renz Farm, a minimum security prison in Missouri, went co-ed, inmates were forbidden to touch each other except during the monthly "dance nights." One such night was recorded by Charlie Nye. "Most of the inmates paired off for the big event," he observed. "Some, however, like James Counce at right, merely sat and listened to the music. He is a married man and did not care to join in."

OVERLEAF: *Bleak surroundings and an even bleaker future were what life held for Bonita Denney and her daughter, Kristy, when Jim Wright found them living in public housing in Chiefland, Florida. Mrs. Denney, terminally ill with leukemia and looking years older than her actual age of only twenty, was trying to get her husband transferred from a prison in Georgia to one in Florida—so that she and her daughter could visit him more easily and so that Kristy could get to know the father she had not seen since infancy. In June, after their story and Wright's photographs appeared in the Gainesville Sun, Bobby Denney was granted a special reprieve and was reunited with his family. In the fall of 1976 the Denneys were divorced; the following January, Bonita Denney died.*

JIM WRIGHT, GAINESVILLE SUN
(FIRST PLACE, PORTRAIT AND PERSONALITY)

BOB BROWN, RICHMOND NEWSPAPERS

In St. Petersburg, Florida, a high flyer (below) and a game senior citizen (opposite) got into the act when Fred Victorin began snapping the shutter. The spry octogenarian, who had been watching the Frisbee throwers from the sidelines, was easily persuaded to try her hand. Another aerial act (right) was captured by Bob Brown.

OVERLEAF: These "good buddies" are, from left: Catfish, the Frito Bandito, Chic-a-dee, Foxy Lady, Black Bear, Sage Brush, Light Buck, and Hot Patch. Proudly displaying their badges, buttons, patches, and "handles," they posed for photographer Charlie Nye during a CB jamboree in Eugene, Oregon, in July, 1976.

CHARLIE NYE, EUGENE REGISTER-GUARD

OPPOSITE AND ABOVE: FRED VICTORIN, ST. PETERSBURG TIMES AND EVENING STANDARD

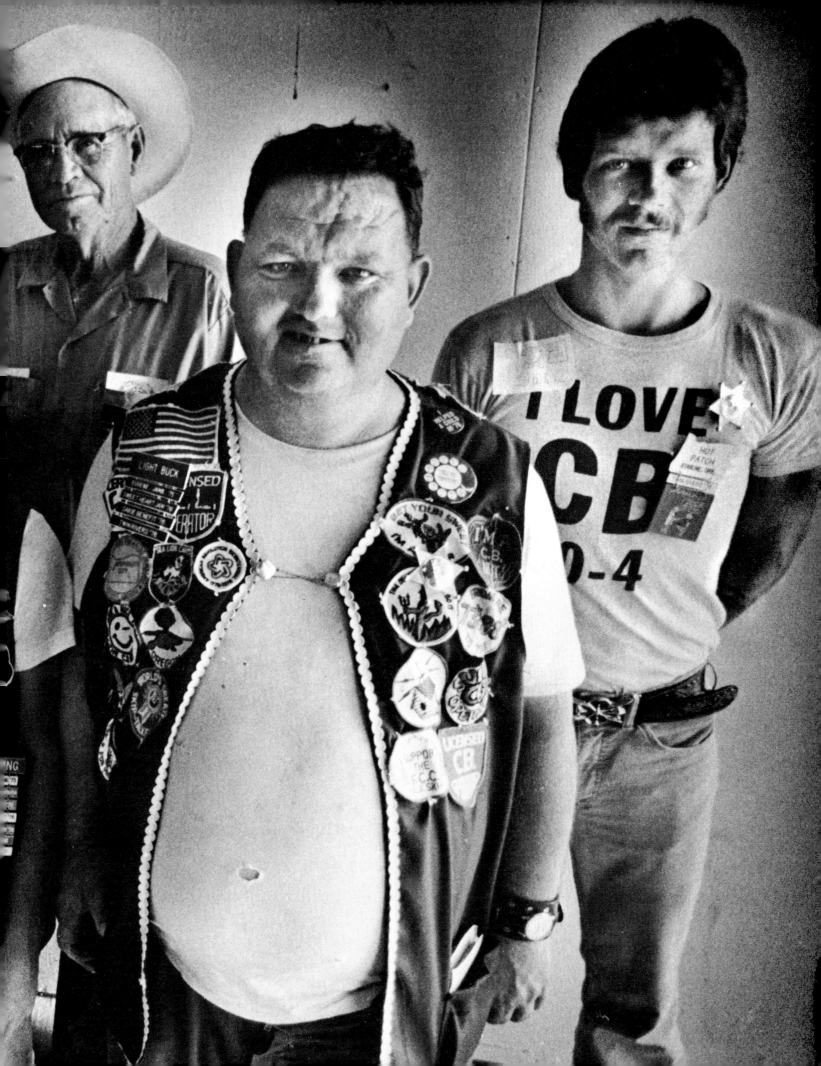

DARRELL DAVIDSON, HOUSTON CHRONICLE (HONORABLE MENTION, PORTRAIT AND PERSONALITY)

Lucille Turner of Houston, Texas, who uses flash cards to teach the deaf how to read lips, held an especially appropriate cue card up for Darrell Davidson when he snapped the picture opposite. William R. Goddard, seen below, insists that the hand-painted signs that line the road in front of his Lakemore, Ohio, home are just a way to have a little fun and wake people up. "If Grandpa can't have a little fun," Goddard says, "what the hell . . . " Just what kind of fun he isn't saying.

DAVID A. ROESE, AKRON BEACON JOURNAL

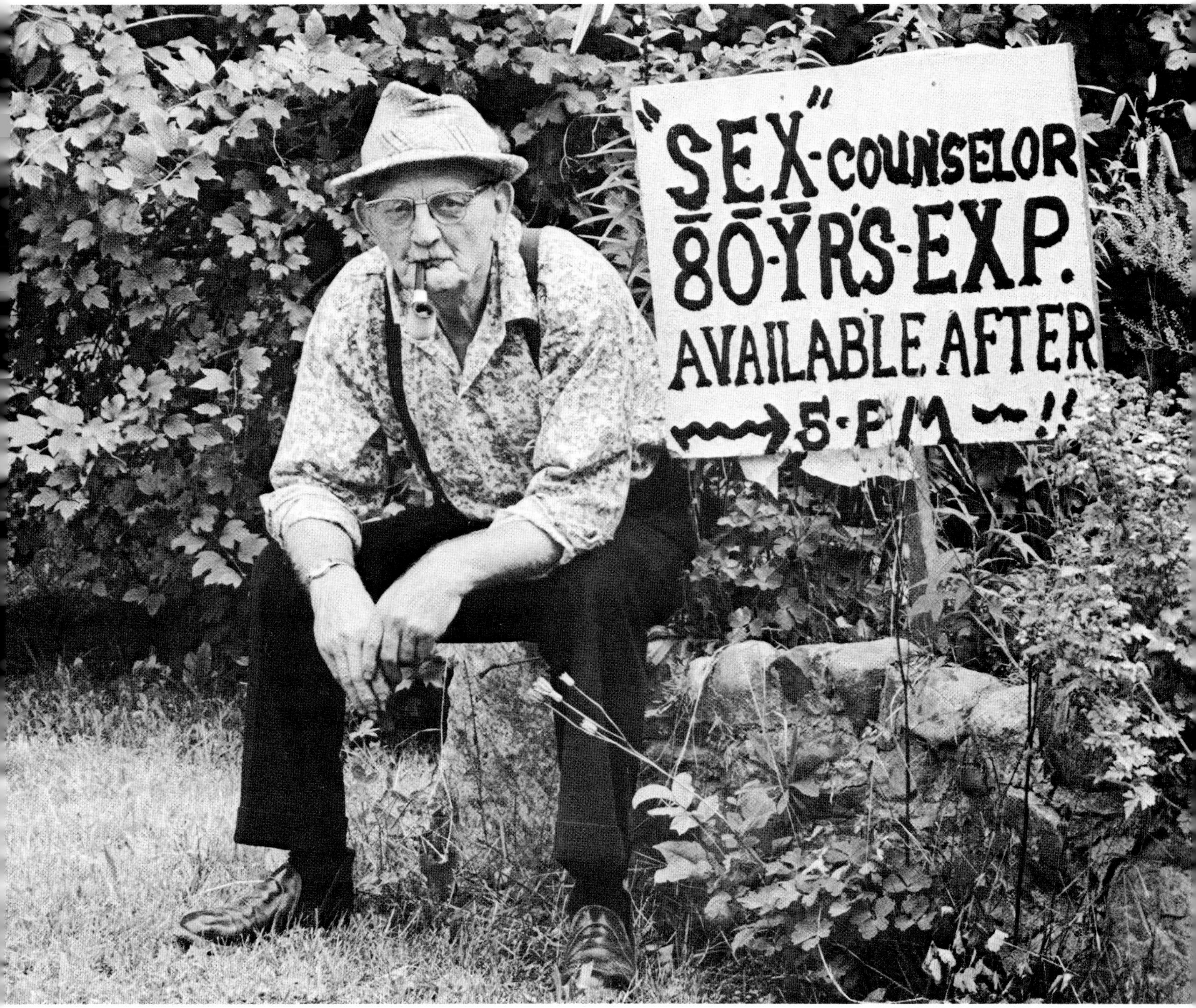

It was a dog-day afternoon: oppressive heat, an implacable sun, and nary a rain cloud in sight. So how to cool a parched lawn without getting overheated oneself? Here's eighty-year-old Catherine Turney's solution.

Gramp

*by Mark and
Dan Jury*

On February 11, 1974, a retired Pennsylvania coal miner named Frank Tugend, aged eighty-one and of dubiously sound mind—albeit of sound body—removed his false teeth and announced that he was no longer going to eat or drink. Three weeks later, to the day, he died. His death brought to a close the Tugend clan's three-year ordeal and ended a three-year effort to document "Gramp" Tugend's gradual, inexorable and, finally, total deterioration. With a camera and tape recorder, Frank Tugend's grandsons, Mark and Dan Jury, had sought to preserve each stage of Gramp's slow submission to senility, that geriatric curse known to medical science as generalized arteriosclerosis. And so they photographed him standing naked before the picture window, and "talking" to the giant red rabbit that he claimed lived in the refrigerator, and sleeping like a small child on the living-room rug. Senility is by no means a unique problem; more than three million American families are dealing with it right now. The Tugends' solution to the problem was to keep Gramp at home, even when it became clear, toward the end, that he might be more readily sustained in a hospital, where he could be fed intravenously. Gramp had made it plain that he wanted to die at home, and so his family permitted him to do so, preserving intact what remained of his dignity. Thereafter Mark and Dan Jury, using the pictures they had taken and the observations and conversations they had recorded on tape, put together the book they call *Gramp*, published by Grossman in 1976. The following photographs are excerpted from that book. During Gramp's final months, when he required almost constant care, the Jury brothers learned a lot about their grandfather, about other members of their family, and about each other. But most of all, they report, they learned a lot about themselves.

Frank Tugend (far left) with Nan, his wife of fifty-seven years, and (again at near left) with his great-granddaughter Hillary, Mark Jury's daughter. A family picnic (below) brings together Dan Jury (far left), Gramp, Nan, great-grandson Joshua, Mark's wife Dee, daughter Florence—called Nink by the family—and Hillary.

OVERLEAF: *Forgetting where his room was located, Gramp would pace incessantly until he was utterly exhausted. Then he would collapse, drifting into a deep sleep wherever he happened to fall. He also became a destructive prankster, dismantling the stove and sticking lit cigars in Nan's sweater drawer.*

"I guess we ain't seen nothing yet," said a member of the family when Gramp was discovered washing his hands in the toilet bowl. When a friend of Nink's stopped by for coffee, Gramp removed his false teeth and passed them to the man saying, "Will you butter this, please?" Even when directed to his room and literally tucked into bed, he would get up during the night and tear the room apart. Bedclothes would be pulled off and strewn everywhere, his dresser would be upended, and all the clothes and other belongings from his closet would be on the floor.

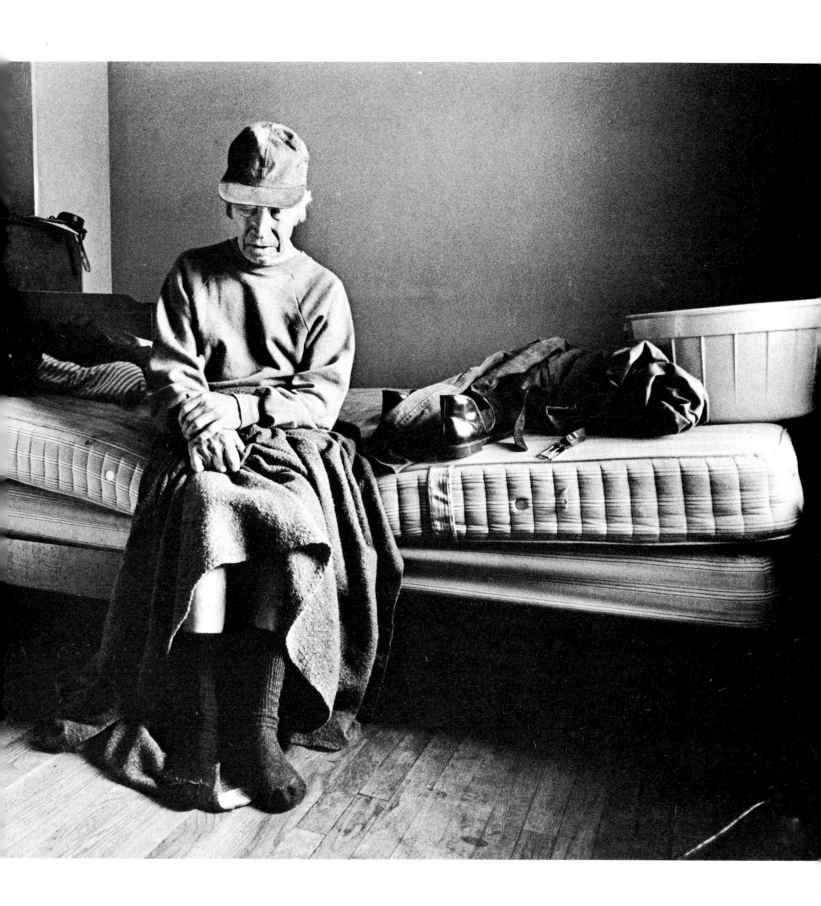

The moment the Tugend family dreaded—but all knew was inevitable—came almost without warning: Gramp lost control of his bowels, and overnight the clan set into action a quasi-military operation involving diapers and pins, rolls of toilet paper, and a well-orchestrated platoon system for getting him cleaned up before the next accident occurred. Then Gramp simply decided to stop eating. Each family member tried to get some food into him, an effort that often proved futile. When, for example, Nink thought that she had persuaded Gramp to take a swallow of high-protein ''astronaut breakfast,'' he suddenly spat the fluid back into the cup and gurgled into it.

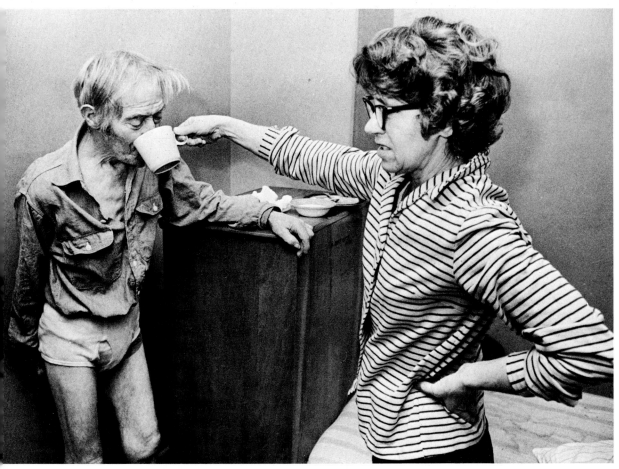

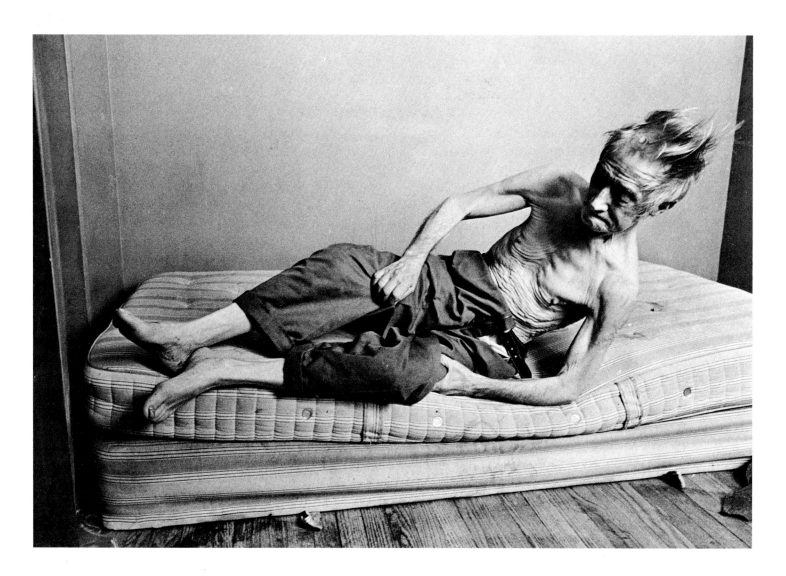

"It is probably the feeling that Gramp is patiently waiting for death that fascinates me the most. He lies there, not stirring, not asking for anything, not even calling for enough substance to keep away the pain of thirst and maybe starvation. . . .Of one thing I am sure. No matter how many times I have to clean Gramp, or feed him, or blow his nose, or care for him in the middle of the night when my body only wants to ignore him, I will always remember the good times with Gramp before I recall the bad."
From Dan Jury's journal
February 23, 1974

As the end approached, Gramp wanted somebody with him all the time; his bony but still strong fingers clutched the hand of whomever was at his bedside. When Dan took his turn Gramp seemed oblivious to the fact that he was in the room, and Dan tried to move his hand away. But the wiry fingers closed and pulled it back. "I went in and held his hand," said Hillary. "He liked me to hold his hand. I thought he was pretty nice and lovable. This is the last day. He died that night."

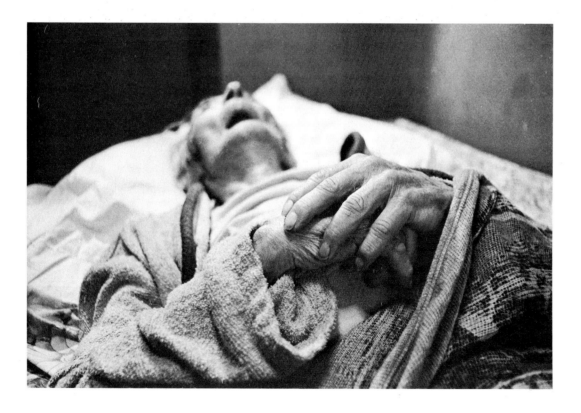

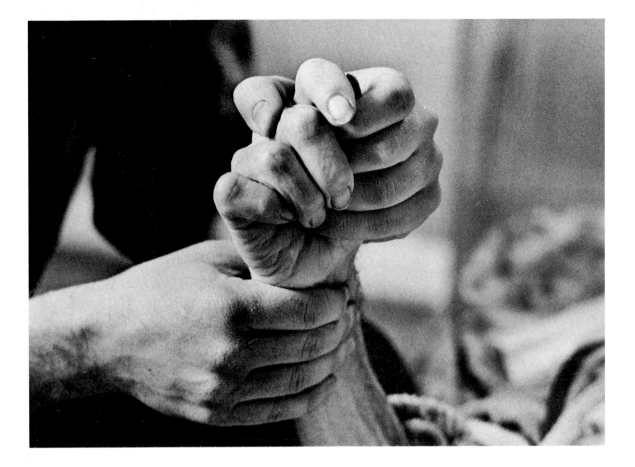

Gramp finally lapsed into a very deep sleep and did not move for nine or ten hours. Mark Jury was sitting at his side when Gramp suddenly became very animated and started to writhe and moan. "I am positive," Mark told Nan, "I just witnessed the spirit or life force or whatever leave Gramp's body." As Mark described the experience, Nink walked into Gramp's room, looked at him and said, "I think Dad's gone."

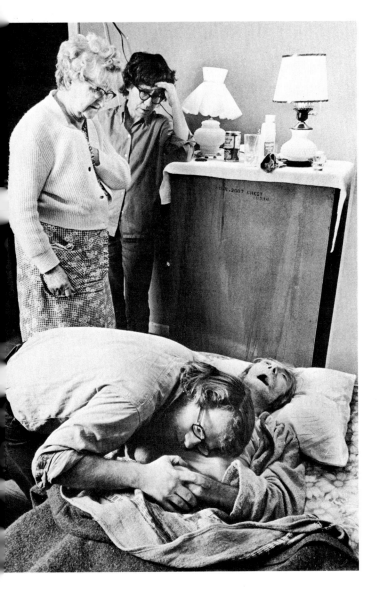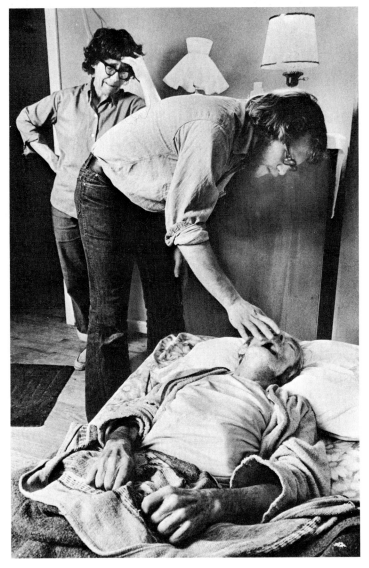

At the very end Mark Jury was to write: "Surprisingly, I felt no overwhelming sense of relief that Gramp was gone; instead a tinge of emptiness, a feeling that we would miss the craziness he brought into our lives—but, most of all, I felt an enormous amount of respect for this tough old coal miner. 'You pulled it off, Gramp. You really pulled it off.'"

Kansas

by Jim Richardson

WORLD UNDERSTANDING CITATION

A Kansan marvels at the ocean, but yearns for the flat land. In the high mountains, he complains that he can't see out. The great canyons are stunning, he'll admit, but they're sterile. In his heart he hungers for fertile earth, for a land that rolls gently and can be worked. He believes in the land and in the future. Kansas has two main products; food, and the next generation. It is not an easy land to love, but things grow on it. Time is measured by the growing, or by the preparations for the growing, or by the harvest of what has grown. The year is marked by spring's first thunderstorm, or by the heading out of the wheat, or by the first killing frost. And always the growing is determined by the weather, for it reigns supreme. Men and women measure the land and the weather, not by its effect on them, but by its effect on their children. That is where their dreams are. And if their children have not been told, they are at least aware that they are the instruments of their parents' dreams— and that colors everything. They must find some way of fulfilling their parents' wishes while at the same time leading a life that is personally satisfying. In a churning mixture of inner drives and desires, and outside pressures and expectations, they strive and rebel, fail and succeed. Finally, on graduation day, they stand together in caps and gowns before the American flag and the admiring eyes of parents and grandparents, siblings and friends. In that gathering place of so many hopes and dreams, a though occurs to them and they grin. They are the new generation. Jim Richardson has been photographing Kansas for five years—and this is the second year that his work has brought him a World Understanding Citation. "When I started photographing my hometown of Belleville," he says, "I was certain of my knowledge of the Kansas people. Now I'm not sure that I know very much at all."

Kansas is a land of simple
foundations. Do not look for
richness quickly, or in established
places. What Kansas has to offer is
often found in virtually unknown
or unnamed places. On July 4,
1976 a grandmother and her
grandaughter stood before a
muraled store in Centralia
(above); a minor event, but
not for the two of them. In
Morganville (right), hollyhocks
grow every year on the corner of
Main Street; planted, perhaps, by
the man who owns the pickup.
The thunderhead (far right)
towering above Maple Hill
appeared dark and ominous from
beneath. But from a few miles to
the west it glistened and soared,
blindingly white.

If you don't meet the people you haven't seen the town. You can't see a community unless you see the residents. If you don't you'll miss Andy Andrews' barber shop in Cuba (top), where you can be confident that your $1.75 will buy a lot of haircutting. Among the memorabilia that cover the walls of Andy's shop are postcards from ham radio buddies around the world. You can drop in any Thursday, Friday, or Saturday —and Andy will even come on Saturday evening if you happen to have to work that day. And don't miss the tavern in Alma (right) or the beer garden at the fair in Belleville (left).

Rossville High School is the repository of the town's dreams. From the outside it appears chaotic and frenetic. But once inside, seeming random activity falls into an intricate pattern of social striving and the search for personal identity. Voting on the prom theme does not strike adults as crucial to happiness (right). But most adults have forgotten how they themselves learned to relate to adults, or how endless an hour class could be, or the time in life when they owned nothing but their name and wanted desperately not to be forgotten.

Sports pervade the school, and therefore the town. On the court, the gridiron, and the diamond are focused the dreams of parents and children. Below, a father-son football event. Being part of the team is belonging. For the team, athletes will endure physical pain and personal humiliation.

For Rossville's seniors, the first day of school (left) is devoted to filling new yearbooks with autographs and felicitous words. The informality of cutoff jeans and tee shirts contrasts sharply with the pomp and ceremony of the last day of school—graduation day (right). Co-salutatorian and student-body president of the class of 1976 LuAnn Miller (below) stood beneath a tree on her family's farm with the box for her gown, which must be returned intact for next year's graduate.

The headlights cut through the gloom as the funeral procession comes out of Rossville (left). The father of one of the high school students has died suddenly. The other students, on the threshold of adulthood, hardly know how to act, let alone how to understand. In Belleville (below), Ralph Fraser, the water witcher, is surrounded in death by those who had surrounded him in life. At the end of the service they walk away—and life abides.

For how many generations have people stood before fires and raised their arms in defiance of their enemies, as Cindy Pugh did on the eve of the Rossville Homecoming game? And for how long have young men like the rodeo contestants below and at left sought to test and demonstrate their strength? If America can be found anywhere, it can be found here, in Kansas.

Appalachia

by Jack Corn

Appalachia first intruded upon America's mass consciousness in 1959, when John Kennedy campaigned through the hills of West Virginia and directed the focus of trailing television crews towards an exploited region whose people, like its coal, had been used—and tossed aside like so much human scoria. At about the same time Jack Corn, then a staff photographer with the *Nashville Tennessean*, began to travel through the mountains with his camera to record on film the life and hard times of the people of Appalachia. The results of his work were so outstanding that Documerica, a federally sponsored project to document environmental problems in the United States, lent its support to Corn's efforts. The photographs reproduced on the following twenty-six pages represent a small portion of Corn's Appalachian portfolio. Much has changed in the mountains since he began to photograph its people and places. In the early 1960's, the region suffered an annual population decline of 120,000 as whole families fled the area in search of employment elsewhere. A huge influx of federal money helped alter that pattern in the 1970's, and then the energy crisis created a heightened demand for coal and a small boom in Appalachia. In 1976 the region produced more than two-thirds of the 665 million tons of coal mined in the United States. But even this new prosperity is a mixed blessing, for coal has been Appalachia's salvation and its scourge. For some, like the miner pictured above, the increased use of coal has meant a steady job and a regular paycheck. For too many others, it has meant seeing land ravaged by strip mines and water poisoned by silt and acid. For Jack Corn, who now teaches photography at West Virginia University, it means that many more people and places to photograph for his ongoing documentation and pictorial history of Appalachia.

Corn took this photograph in 1965 between Clairfield, Tennessee, and Middlesboro, Kentucky, an area perhaps best described by Thomas E. Gish, editor and publisher of The Mountain Eagle in Whitesburg, Kentucky. "The Central Appalachian area where I am from is one of the leading poverty centers in the entire country. Incomes average less than half the national average. The educational system is the nation's worst. More than a third of the housing is classified as substandard. The creeks and hollows are filled with maimed and broken people. The hillsides are being gutted by strip mines, and the creeks are filling with rocks and mud. If there is any place in the United States that is a total mess, it is the Appalachian coal fields."

WASP has become an American acronym synonymous with success. To be born a white, Anglo-Saxon Protestant is to be born into the nation's power elite—and automatically a member of the ruling class. The people pictured on these pages are WASP's. Their Scotch-Irish ancestors settled in Appalachia during the eighteenth century and some of the houses they live in date back to that period. Jack Corn shot the photographs on these pages between 1959 and

1973, when Appalachia was languishing in the doldrums of the recession. The descendants of people who had fought in the American Revolution clung tenaciously to their homes, land, and culture even though there was not enough work, not enough money, not enough food, not enough of anything except time to think about how things used to be or could be if the mines opened up again. Until they did, there was nothing much to do except wait.

Hunger was a painful enemy of the children of Appalachia when Corn took these pictures in the early 1960's. One mountain man had this to tell a reporter when asked about the problem: "No, sir, none of the children get their lunch at school. The well-off kids from town, they bring their money and so they get fed. It don't mean nothing to the parents, a few dollars here or there. But I can't give each of the kids a quarter a day. I don't have it; I don't have one quarter, never mind six of them. So, they just sit there while the others eat. Sometimes a kid will offer them something he doesn't want to eat, and sometimes my kids are too proud to accept, but sometimes they swallow their pride and get some of that soup they have."

Back in 1947, about 450,000 men worked in Appalachia's coal mines. Then cheap natural gas stole coal's home-heating market and railroads converted to diesel locomotives. By 1964 the number of men employed in the mines had fallen to 150,000. Over the past few years the demand for coal has begun rising again, and Appalachian coal production is supposed to increase from the current rate of 420 million tons a year to about one billion tons annually by 1990. With increased demand and production there is little room for operations like the "doghole" mine at near right. Back in 1964, it was a two-man, one-mule operation.

OVERLEAF: *Strip mining produces long trainloads of coal but leaves behind torn and devastated landscapes like this one.*

Clean, drinkable water, like the kind carried in half-gallon milk jugs by these miners (right) is often a precious commodity in Appalachia. Two of the major health problems in the region are intestinal parasites—contracted by drinking unsanitary water—and rotting teeth—a consequence of the soda-pop habit that children acquire at age two because the water is to be avoided. An estimated 10,000 miles of streams and creeks in Appalachia have been fouled by acid runoffs from the strip mines. And when a stream is poisoned, the land around it dies, too. Householders who once got fresh vegetables from small backyard gardens now stand by helplessly while plants wither and die, killed by poison effluent from the mines.

The only alternative to strip mining is deep-shaft mining, which is harder, more dangerous, and more expensive. The men at left are headed down into a pit in New Richlands, Virginia. Once underground, men must perform hard physical labor in dark, cramped quarters (above and below). Says one miner, "Sure conditions in the mines are better than they used to be. Sure we're making more money in the mines. But things were so bad they had to get better, and they sure as hell better continue to get better if people want this damn coal. We pay a helluva price diggin' it, and the people better be prepared to pay more if they want it."

Miners risk cave-ins, explosions, black-lung disease, and a variety of other dangers to get their hands on the valuable black lumps (below) that may help solve our energy crisis. After a hard day underground, a miner (right) rests for a moment before heading home. Slung over his shoulder is the battery pack that powers his headlamp.

The recipe for Appalachian moonshine has remained unchanged for over a century. First corn meal is scalded and allowed to cool in a large wooden container. Then water and ground malt are added, followed by two pounds of sugar for every one pound of corn. The mixture, known as still beer, is allowed to ferment for six days in the containers (top). A coiled metal tube (left) is then placed in an oil drum and the mixture is distilled into clear "white lightning" (right). The two miners opposite seem to prefer a milder brew.

153

Just going to school can be a
chore in Appalachia. Jack Corn
photographed these children
(left) in 1964, as they trudged four
miles over muddy mountain roads
to reach their one-room school
near Clairfield, Tennessee.
The schoolhouse had no
formal playground or athletic
equipment, so the kids invented
their own games, like the contest
of jumping sticks below.

One teacher, six grades, and no frills, that's the kind of school Jack Corn focused on in these pictures taken in Crawford, Tennessee. An astonishing fifty percent of the young men who came up through a similar system in Harlan County, Kentucky, during this period failed the U.S. Army's mental tests. When one passed, it was cause for celebration. "I got one that made it," said one proud mountain mother. "How he did it was this. He would quit out of school two or three days to earn money to pay for lunches and things like that. Hit took him an extry year, but we was all real happy for him when he passed for the Army."

"Bloody Harlan" it was called in 1931, after five strikers were killed. Then in 1973 the Harlan County miners struck again (left) and this time they remained out for a year in a bitter and often violent labor dispute. The union never did manage to organize some of the mines, as the pensionless old miner above knows all too well.

OVERLEAF: *Since 1839, 120,000 miners have died in mine accidents. Pictured are friends, fellow miners, relatives, and rescue workers gathered in the early morning mist and fog after a 1966 mine disaster in Brimstone, Tennessee, that claimed five lives.*

Not many survive as long as old
"Bear" Phillips (left), a retired
mine worker photographed in his
home by Jack Corn in 1972. If
disease or the mines don't prove
fatal, the violent ways of the
mountain people themselves can
end a life too soon. Such was the
case when Corn took the picture
at right, in 1971: relatives had just
finished digging a grave for a
young man who lost an argument
with a gun. The violence is still
there, but on the whole, life in
the region would seem to be
improving. Conditions in the
mines have gotten better, pay is
higher than ever before, and
although inflation takes a big
chunk out of every miner's
paycheck, better facilities
promise a brighter future for the
children growing up in the hills
and valleys called Appalachia.

Feature Stories

BRUCE BISPING, MINNEAPOLIS TRIBUNE
(NEWSPAPER PHOTOGRAPHER OF THE YEAR)

If anything can truly compete with the concentrated power of a single photo-graph it is, almost certainly, a series of visually arresting images, composed to tell a story. It is sometimes argued that the very best photographs tell an en-tire tale in a single image. This is indisputably true of the compelling candid seen above, which Bruce Bisping calls "The Hurt of a Broken Family" and which was part of the portfolio that won him the Newspaper Photographer of the Year award. But life in all its complexity often defies ready explanation or encapsulation, and it is here that the storytelling aspect of photojournalism comes to the fore. Consider, for example, Chuck McGowen's shot on page 167 of Rev. Sun Myung Moon bestowing his benediction upon the thousands of faithful who turned out for his God Bless America Festival in Yankee Stadium. The impact of Rev. Moon's crusade is best expressed not in his benign postur-ing—reminiscent of countless politicos on uncounted podiums—but in the rapt expressions he elicits from his youthful followers and the intense animos-ity he engenders in others. On pages 166-169 McGowen has given us those reactions as well. It is precisely this interplay of emotions that amplifies Bill Wunsch's study of a dramatic white-water rescue from a raging torrent high in the Rocky Mountains (pages 176-177), and it is that same quality, on a less dra-matic but no less poignant scale, that gives special resonance to Ethan Hoff-man's chronicle of a collapsed marriage, "I Divorce You, I Divorce You, I Di-vorce You" (pages 196-207). From bucolic idyll to big-city trauma unit, from the Pecos to the Potomac, from the rainforests of the Amazon to the coal fields of West Virginia, these feature stories are a record of hope and folly, high drama and high jinks. They range from the mundane to the monumental, and touch all aspects of the human condition in between.

Although Rev. Sun Myung Moon's attempt to jump on the Bicentennial bandwagon was thwarted when official sanction for his God Bless America Festival in New York City's huge Yankee Stadium was withdrawn, his youthful followers (left and below) remained undaunted. What did faze them were the thunderstorms that drenched the city and stadium on the night of the festival, keeping all but 30,000 of the faithful away. Before Rev. Moon finished speaking (right), smoke bombs exploded and half the crowd left.

CHUCK McGOWEN, WILMINGTON NEWS-JOURNAL

Moon's most vocal detractors have been the small but persistent group of parents who charge him and his Unification Church with the kidnapping (right, below) and brainwashing (far right) of their children. They liken Moon to a Hitler of the seventies (left) and have pressed the I.R.S. for an investigation of the church's tax-exempt multimillion-dollar holdings. Rev. Moon controls a conglomerate of South Korean industries, and his American disciples (above) bring in an estimated $12 million a year in personal contributions and solicited donations.

JAMES PARCELL, THE WASHINGTON POST (THIRD PLACE, NEWS PICTURE STORY)

Enveloped in dense, black smoke and clutching her infant daughter, Marie Ateba (far left) leans out the window of her blazing apartment. Beside her on the window ledge, his arms dangling limply toward the courtyard four stories below, is her unconscious four-year-old son. Firemen reach her by ladder (near left), and she passes the children to them before going down the ladder herself. Once on the ground (below), Mrs. Ateba anxiously looks on as firemen rescue a third child from the burning building.

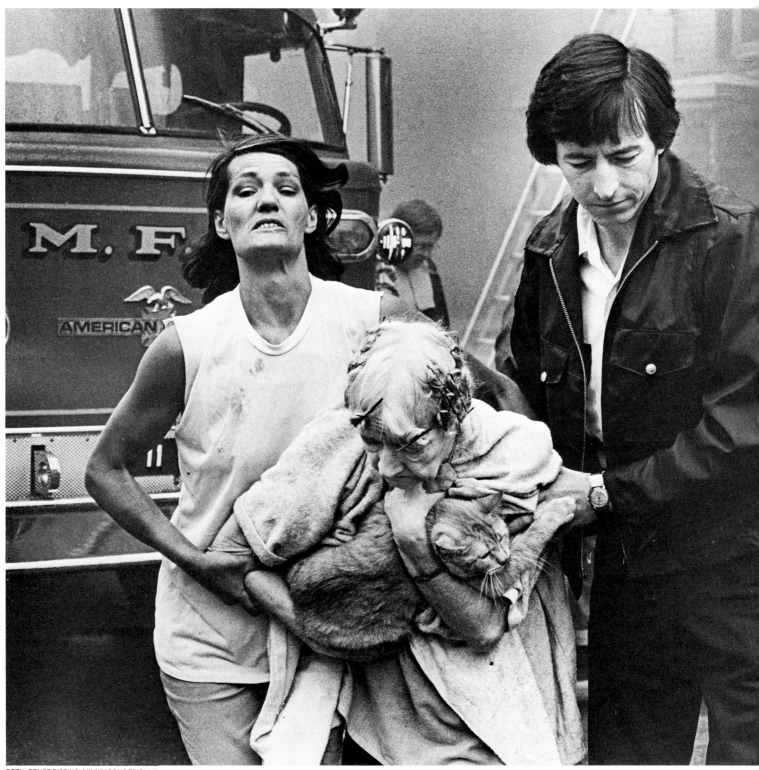

BOTH: BRUCE BISPING, MINNEAPOLIS TRIBUNE

Bruce Bisping took both of these photographs at Minneapolis fires. At left, an aged woman clutches her cat, the only thing she saved when fire gutted the tenement where she lived. Below, an exhausted fireman rests after battling flames in a southern Minneapolis apartment.

BORIS YARO, LOS ANGELES TIMES (SECOND PLACE, NEWS PICTURE STORY)

Shortly after takeoff from the Hollywood-Burbank Airport, a DC-6 on a training flight developed serious trouble. A defective propeller came loose and wrenched off the number-three engine just as the aircraft left the runway, forcing the pilot to put down on a nearby golf course. The plane skidded to a halt and all five passengers scrambled to safety as firemen applied foam (left) as a precaution against fire. Using a special saw, they tried to cut through the fuselage to the crew—but sparks from the saw ignited a puddle of gasoline lying beneath the foam (left, below). Within seconds, the DC-6 and nine firemen were ablaze (below). Autopsies later revealed that the crew members the firemen were attempting to save had died on impact.

Driving along the tortuous
mountain roads that traverse the
Rockies is always hazardous, but
in the spring it becomes doubly
treacherous. Then melting snow
and heavy rains turn mountain
streams into whitecap-flecked
torrents. On such a day, a steering
malfunction in the automobile
Leslie Cady was driving sent her
car rolling down a thirty-foot

embankment and into the swollen, turbulent waters of Clear Creek. Luckily, the car landed right-side up in water that was only as deep as the door handles (above). But because of the swiftness of the current, the rescue of Mrs. Cady and her two young daughters by wetsuit-clad firemen (left and right) was to take almost two hours.

William Obera couldn't stand the thought that his estranged wife, Sadie, might someday live with another man. So he took her hostage, and both of them died after an hour-long confrontation with police in the parking lot of the San Bernardino hospital where she was employed. In the photograph at far left, Obera shouts at police as they begin to surround him from behind parked cars. In the third photograph, a policeman's bullet strikes Obera in the chest and he begins to fall. Still holding onto his wife's uniform, he rams the gun into her abdomen (final frame)—and fires. He died within minutes, she several hours later.

Jesse Rodriguez had been ice fishing on Quarry Lake in Racine, Wisconsin, for about two hours when, feeling the cold, he set out across the spring-fed lake to gather some firewood. About one hundred feet from shore the ice began to crack—and from the safety of the bank Charles S. Vallone recorded the rescue efforts that ensued. At near right, Rodriguez lies flat and attempts to distribute his weight evenly, but the ice continues to crumble. After lying in the icy water for almost an hour, Rodriguez is reached by firemen who toss him a rope and drag him ashore just as the ice gives way completely.

CHARLES S. VALLONE, RACINE JOURNAL-TIMES (HONORABLE MENTION, NEWS PICTURE STORY)

The monks of St. John's Abbey in Collegeville, Minnesota, defy stereotype. All are members of the Benedictine order and gather together several times a day for communal prayers and meals, but otherwise their activities vary. Some are carpenters; monks, for example, constructed the pews opposite. Others are composers and theologians and many teach at adjoining St. John's University. They are no longer required to wear the habit, and blue jeans and sneakers (below) are not uncommon attire.

During a six-week ROTC program at Ft. Knox, women trained with men. They marched, used guns, and participated in simulated combat situations—where the woman at left, below, crooked her finger to urge her comrades on. According to male cadets, the co-ed army is a more relaxed one. Drill sergeants have cleaned up their language and are more soft-spoken—although the one below does not appear to have changed much. Both sexes agree that women aren't yet equal in strength and endurance (left, above) and the latrines have yet to be liberated (right).

BRYAN MOSS, LOUISVILLE COURIER-JOURNAL

On a hot July day in Lane County, Oregon, Linda McCarthy decided to put to the test an obscure local ordinance that permits topless sunbathing—and makes no distinction as to the sex of the bather. The woman in the background was not amused.

Sarah Caldwell was energetically guest-conducting the Minnesota Orchestra in the initial minutes of a two-hour rehearsal when her glasses started to fall (far right). The indomitable director of the Boston Opera Company flicked them back on without missing a beat. Below she pauses to tell the orchestra, "That place demands more accent."

JIM MCTAGGART, THE MINNEAPOLIS STAR

Although separated by a continent, the boys in these pictures share a fascination, as most boys do, with guns, warfare, and violence—providing that the guns are toys, the warfare just a game, and the violence purely imaginary. The kids on the left were photographed in Golden, Colorado, by Eric Bakke. He reports that they are schoolmates who get together often in their makeshift headquarters to plan and reenact battles of the past. The boys on the right were photographed in Samoset, Florida, by Dick Bell.

OPPOSITE: ERIC BAKKE, GOLDEN DAILY TRANSCRIPT; ABOVE AND FOLLOWING: DICK BELL, ST. PETERSBURG TIMES

According to photographer Dick Bell, the Florida boys in these pictures were pretending to be a police S.W.A.T. team, having been inspired by the television program of that name. "I was driving around looking for pictures when I saw these kids playing," he said. "I wasn't thinking about making a big statement about guns, I just showed what boys do naturally."

Terry Lee Harmon and his wife, Denise, had been married about a month when, after an argument over their Corvette, Mrs. Harmon hopped into the car and began to drive away. Harmon jumped on the hood in an attempt to stop her, but to no avail. Instead of halting, she obstinately drove eight miles to police headquarters with her husband clinging tenaciously to the hood. Police officers' futile attempts to make peace ended with both husband and wife being charged with disorderly conduct.

DEAN D. DIXON, MOBILE PRESS REGISTER (HONORABLE MENTION, SPOT NEWS)

ETHAN HOFFMAN, COLUMBIA MISSOURIAN (HONORABLE MENTION, FEATURE PICTURE STORY/MAG)

When first we met we did not guess
That Love would prove so hard a master;
Of more than common friendliness
When first we met we did not guess.
Who could foretell this sore distress,
This irretrievable disaster
When first we met?—We did not guess
That Love would prove so hard a master.
                    Robert Bridges

In twelve years of marriage John and Ellen Hungerford adopted four children, had two of their own, and got involved in a program for problem teenagers. As they became more wrapped up in the children, they gave less to each other. Somewhere along the way they just stopped loving each other. On February 9, 1976, they were divorced. Although John acknowledged that his marriage was finished, he did not want to give up his family—but, as Ellen says, "Where do you divide children, how do you divide children, or do you divide children?" Above, clockwise: Ellen, Matt, Greg, Andy, Clare, Johnny, and Sara.

In an unusual arrangement, John
and Ellen decided to divide their
children. The three eldest are with
John in Kansas City, the three
youngest are with Ellen (above) in
Columbia, Missouri, where she is
completing a degree in art
education. But the entire family
gets together several times a
month, either in Kansas City or
Columbia. Opposite: Ellen sets
the dinner table in anticipation of
one such family reunion.

Being a full-time student and mother is difficult for Ellen, who tries to spend as much time with her children as possible. Despite problems, her outlook regarding her family remains optimistic. "There are still things that were good in that marriage and that will carry through. We have two families now, and each of our families will still share a lot of what was good, and will still remember a lot of what was good. And for each family, it's a time to go on."

John and five of his six chidren are
shown above in a family portrait
taken when his two daughters
were visiting from Columbia. He
speaks candidly about the failure
of his marriage: "I'm not blaming
anybody, but in essence we are
both very, very loving people. We
are both giving people, and we
gave all our love and all our
givingness to everyone around
us except each other."

202

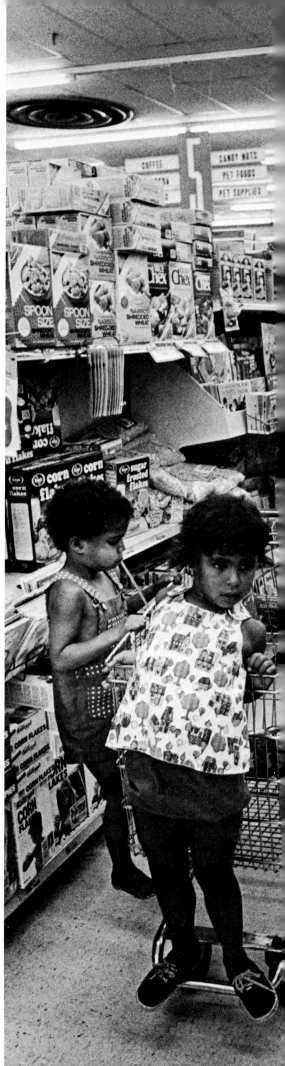

John's daily chores—grocery shopping, preparing meals, doing the dishes and the laundry—are multiplied by three on those weekends when Clare, Sara, and Matt visit, and he must struggle to keep from being completely overwhelmed. Like Ellen, he remains positive in his outlook despite the difficulties inherent in raising two families: "You know, because our family is split up, because I've got the boys and I'm here, and she's got the other three, does that mean it won't work? No, it's different, it could be a little more difficult, but as far as what it takes to raise happy children, there is no formula. Mommy and daddy living happily ever after is no guarantee at all."

205

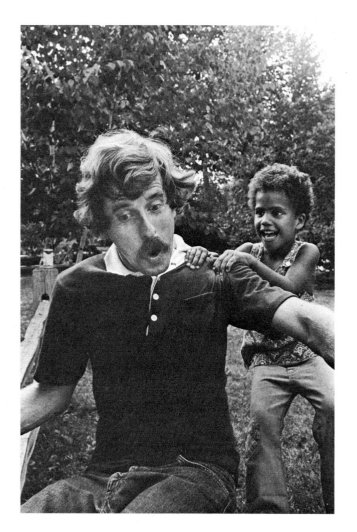

John is deeply committed to his children and spends as much time with them as he can. But being a parent is not only play (above); because John is also the chief disciplinarian around the house (opposite). "I just think there's a responsibility towards the children," he says. "You've made a commitment, and I think no matter what happens you've got to honor that commitment, even more so than the marriage."

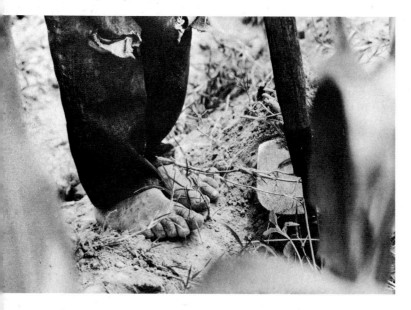

At eighty-eight, Carolinas Peyton (opposite) can fairly say that he has lived a full life. Several lives, in fact. Kidnapped at ten by Chesapeake Bay watermen, Peyton began a long career as a merchant seaman that eventually took him around the world. He also worked as a blacksmith in Sweden and as a sparring partner for Jack Johnson before returning to Rosier Creek on the banks of the Potomac—where, for the last half century, he has tilled the soil and tended the team of mules he uses to work his small farm.

JAMES L. STANFIELD, NATIONAL GEOGRAPHIC
(FIRST PLACE, FEATURE PICTURE STORY/MAG)

Carolinas Peyton not only built the house in which he lives (right), he also felled the timber and shaped the boards himself. His fifty-acre subsistance farm boasts a large flock of chickens, watched over like a hawk by Payton's lone daughter, Lydia Franklin. (In the photograph at left, Mrs. Franklin has just dispatched a chicken hawk that was also watching over the flock.) Peyton takes life easier now, spending a good part of each day with his great-grandson Thomas (below) and the chickens.

212

In a string of primitive settlements that dot both sides of the long common border between Venezuela and Brazil live 15,000 Yanomamo tribesmen, whose way of life has changed little in ten millennia. There is a chronic shortage of marriageable females among the Yanomamo, and this has led the physically strong and politically powerful to prey upon the weaker members of the tribe. A man is judged by the number of women of childbearing age that he is able to take and hold, which explains why the young girl at left—who may be no more than twelve years old—has already become a chieftain's third wife. At right, a malaria victim is held aloft by shamen, all deeply affected by hallucinogens. They wait for the gods of the forest to come forth to exorcise the evil spirit that lurks within the sick man's body.

Photographer Blair Pittman, who was raised near Pecos, Texas, was vacationing west of the Pecos when he came across this old, abandoned railroad station. Once a stop for the Pecos Valley Special—known locally as the Pea Vine Special—it stands today as faded testimony to the glory days of the railroads.

BLAIR PITTMAN, HOUSTON CHRONICLE (THIRD PLACE, FEATURE PICTURE STORY)

These photographs, all taken by James L. Stanfield, demonstrate what pollutants have done to the north branch of the Potomac, where that historic waterway begins its 382-mile run from the Maryland-West Virginia border to Chesapeake Bay. The northern branch area is coal country, and effluent-laden wastes from the mines mix with the river water, producing mud flats such as those seen at far left and killing fish (near left). Seeping acid trickles down into creeks like Mill Run (below), depositing yellow stains.

OVERLEAF: *Just above Washington, D.C., the Potomac River narrows from a width of more than 2,000 feet to less than 200 feet—and crashes through great masses of rock to form Great Falls.*

It is a wet and dreary night near Washington, D.C. At 7:20, as cars speed along a slippery stretch of highway, there is a sudden, stomach-churning screech of brakes. Glass shatters, metal crumples, and a body is broken. Six minutes later rescue workers, accompanied by photographer James L. Stanfield, are on the scene—and while Stanfield takes these remarkable pictures, they go to work (left). The car's driver is bleeding badly and he has lost consciousness. "Looks like one for shock-trauma," says a member of the rescue crew. A call goes out to the Maryland Institute for Emergency Medicine, located in downtown Baltimore. Two Maryland state troopers receive the urgent message and leave immediately for the accident scene in their helicopter (above). They arrive at 7:48. In three minutes the victim is airborne.

221

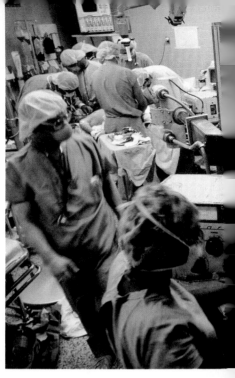

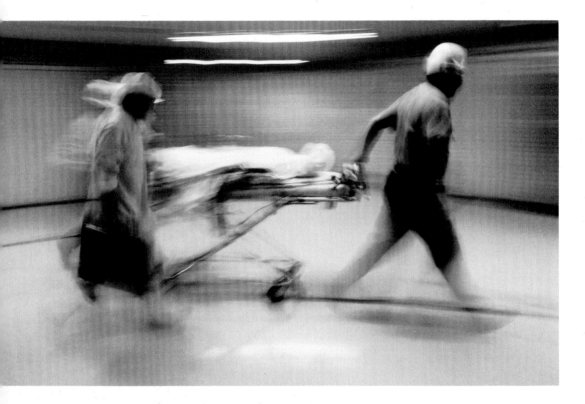

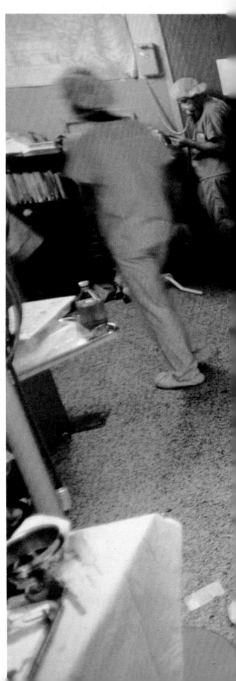

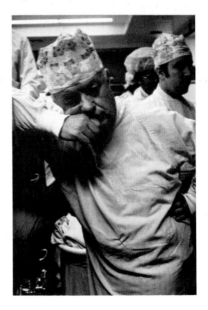

By 8:11 the accident victim has arrived at the institute and is rushed to an operating room (above). The center has four teams that rotate on twenty-four-hour shifts. Doctors and medical students work together on each of these crews, and every member has special training in the care of shock-trauma patients. A neurosurgeon is called to check the patient's head injury while one doctor tries to stanch the bleeding and another begins a blood transfusion. Assistants take X rays of the injured man's spine and leg. Opportunities for a breather (left) are rare indeed.

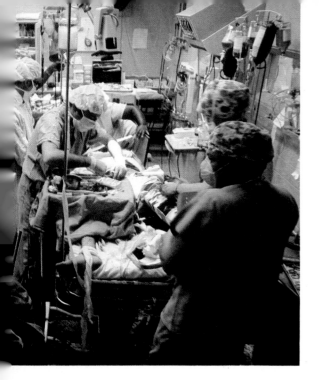

Less than an hour after his accident, the patient is in surgery (left). When he wakes up ten hours later, his head is bandaged and one leg is in a cast—but he is going to recover. Indeed, just five days later he will be well enough to go home. Eight out of ten of the patients brought to the shock-trauma center do go home, a record of which center director Dr. R. Adams Cowley is justifiably proud. "We're knocking the socks off the death rate in this state," he says with a grin.

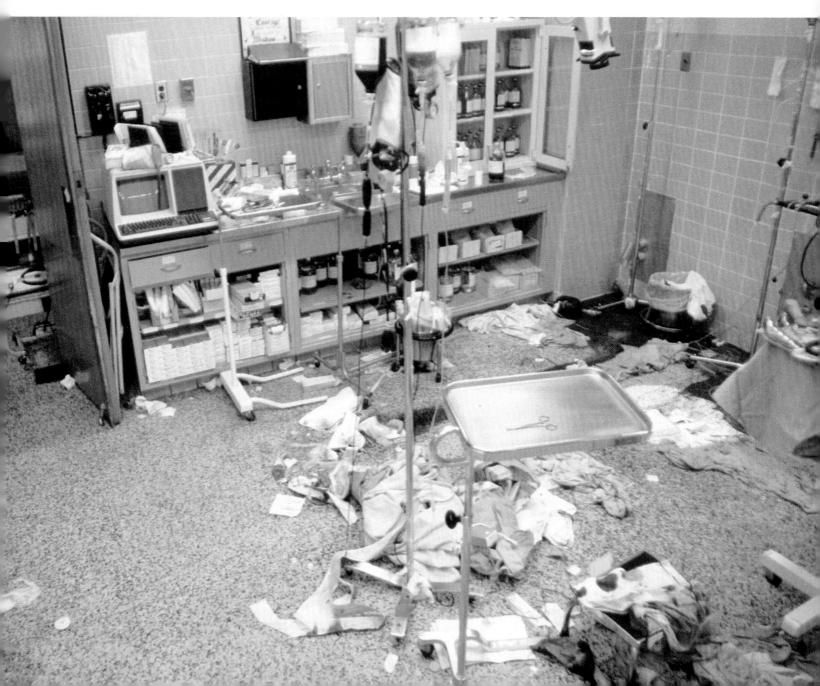

When Carol Bain and her brothers reached high-school age, their father, a West Virginia coal miner, moved the family to Indiana. He did so, he said, to keep his sons out of the mines. In time all of the children married, and one by one all of them returned to the coal fields of West Virginia—including Carol, who recently became that state's first female miner. Her hiring stirred some resentment initially—coworkers' wives picketed the mine entrance during her first week on the job—but Carol's performance has received uniformly high marks. "She works just as hard as the rest of us," says veteran miner David "Hoot" Frost, pictured with Carol at left after their midnight to eight A.M. shift. "Don't know how she keeps her face so clean," he adds with a grin while watching the scene at right.

JODI COBB, NATIONAL GEOGRAPHIC (FIRST PLACE, PORTRAIT AND PERSONALITY/MAG)

Sports

RICH FRISHMAN, PIONEER PRESS
(FIRST PLACE, SPORTS FEATURE)

Breathes there a coach with manner so mellowed that he has never bellowed like the enraged molder of youthful character above, caught in a moment of open-mouthed fury by photographer Rich Frishman. While coaches were yelling, athletes were coming up with some brilliant performances in 1976. Two of the year's most spectacular, caught by Associated Press photographer Eddie Adams, were that of Olympic decathlon champion Bruce Jenner (page 229) and Nadia Comaneci (page 235), a fourteen-year-old of pixie proportions who displaced Olga Korbut as queen of the gymnasts. Muscles captured the public imagination last year, especially those on the body of Arnold Schwarzenegger, who flexed his before an attentive audience (which included photographer Co Rentmeester) in New York's Whitney Museum. For a different kind of excitement a group of motorcyclists got together on a wet and muddy afternoon in Pontiac, Michigan. Also present was photographer Barry Edmonds, who returned with the short but thrilling photo essay on page 236. Flint Born wandered into a Des Moines, Iowa, boxing club one day and by the time he was ready to leave he had recorded on film the moving story of a young boxer trying to punch his way out of the ghetto. Equally moving is Dane Peterson's picture essay about a no-longer-young athlete who dreams of past glories. Then there are times when sports is a laughing matter, as Ron Edmonds clearly demonstrates in his series of shots of a Hawaiian little league umpire—and as Melissa Farlow further emphasizes with her photo of five young ballplayers during a seventh-inning stretch. The combined efforts of these photographers add an extra dimension both to the athletes and to the multitudinous sporting events they were involved in, a dimension that often eludes the naked eye and is seldom seen on commercial television.

JOHN METZGER, SAN BERNARDINO SUN-TELEGRAM (HONORABLE MENTION, SPORTS FEATURE)

You don't laugh at Superman's long johns, you don't spit into the wind, and you don't mess around with Ms. Billie Jean King, even if you are a tennis judge. Although she lost her point here, King went on to win both her match and the Federation Cup Tournament. Bruce Jenner (opposite) was a big winner at the twenty-first modern Olympic Games, held in Montreal during the summer of 1976. Jenner, shown completing a discus throw, thrilled a vast television audience with his gold medal-winning efforts in the grueling two-day decathlon.

EDDIE ADAMS, ASSOCIATED PRESS (FIRST PLACE, SPORTS ACTION/MAG)

KEN REGAN, CAMERA 5

Sweating, straining, grunting, and groaning, Vasily Alekseyev (far left) uses every muscle in his solid, 345-pound body to lift a 408-pound barbell over his head. The effort set a new Olympic record in the weightlifting competition's superheavyweight division and won a gold medal for the thirty-four-year-old Russian, who is considered the world's strongest man. Cuba's Gerardo Fernandez (above) tried to wrest that title away from Alekseyev, but for all his obvious lung power Fernandez was unable to raise the barbell over his head. All the lifter at near left seems to care about is that the barbell he's just released doesn't land on his toes.

ERNEST SCHWORCK, UPI (SECOND PLACE, SPORTS ACTION)

In what may be the beginning of a new art form, twenty-eight-year-old Arnold Schwarzenegger displays his body, which has earned him the title of Mr. Universe five separate times, before an enraptured audience at New York's Whitney Museum. For those interested in vital statistics, the Austrian body builder stands 6-foot-2-inches, weighs 210 pounds, and has a 57-inch chest, 22-inch biceps, a 31-inch waist, 28-inch thighs and 20-inch calves.

BRUCE BISPING, MINNEAPOLIS TRIBUNE

Is that a smile or a grimace on Olga Korbut's face (far right) as she gazes up at Nadia Comaneci, the fourteen-year-old Romanian gymnast who was the undisputed female star of the 1976 Olympic Games? Nadia was, in a word, perfection. No one, man or woman, had ever scored a perfect ten in Olympic gymnastic competition; Comaneci did it seven times, four times on the uneven bars and three times on the balance beam. Was it the wildly cheering crowds that influenced the judges who handed out those unprecedented scores? When asked that very question, former American champion Cathy Rigby Mason said, "If Nadia were doing what she's been doing all alone in an empty room, I'd still have to say that she would get the tens."

EDDIE ADAMS, ASSOCIATED PRESS (FIRST PLACE, SPORTS FEATURE/MAG)

Evel Knievel he's not, but sixteen-year-old Danny Wright did a death-defying routine worthy of the master during this motorcycle race in Pontiac, Michigan. Losing control of his bike (above), Wright did a somersault into the middle of a very muddy track. The next rider, coming up fast, reared back quickly (near right) and just managed to avoid hitting Wright. Miraculously, the cycle's rear wheel missed the downed cyclist's head by inches—and seconds later Wright crawled off the track (far right), none the worse for wear except for a slightly sore wrist. As a matter of fact, photographer Barry Edmonds reports that Wright returned to compete that night.

BARRY EDMONDS, FLINT JOURNAL (FIRST PLACE, SPORTS PICTURE STORY)

The men in helmets and ice skates below are faced with a problem that constantly confronts hockey players around the world. Should they dash out across the ice to join their teammates in the brawl, or should they stay where they are, making certain that nobody skates off with all those expensive gloves and sticks.

FLINT BORN, DES MOINES REGISTER (HONORABLE MENTION, SPORTS PICTURE STORY)

Photographer Flint Born came across the Des Moines, Iowa, boxing club seen at right quite by chance—and decided to spend the day there, shooting men like Muhammed ''Bull Moose'' Hunley (far right) in pursuit of their dreams. "I'm tired of living in the ghetto, man," Hunley informed Born—and so he has decided to punch his way out. Several times a week he shows up at the gloomy basement club, which contains little more than a ring, tape for his hands (above), and a few old and well-worn punching bags hanging from the ceiling. Not much, but for a thirty-year-old middleweight like Hunley it is the sort of place where dreams like the one he harbors might just come true.

Nearly every night David Shrader sits in his Topeka, Kansas, home and leafs through his well-worn scrapbook, staring at pictures of a strong young man wearing a Kansas State Teachers College track suit. Shrader was a young shot-putter and hammer thrower when the photographs were taken—and today, sixty-two years old, overweight and out of condition, he still is. He's been successful throwing the weights and has the trophies to prove it, along with a picture of himself as a robust middle-aged athlete that stands behind the mementos. Although his once-powerful body has begun to fail him, Shrader still works out with a homemade hammer and remembers how things used to be.

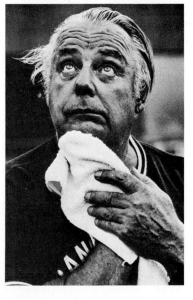

DAVID PETERSON, TOPEKA CAPITAL-JOURNAL (SECOND PLACE, SPORTS PICTURE STORY)

244

Sometimes sports is all fun and games, like disappearing into a dark cloud of dust to avoid the catcher's tag at home plate (left). Then there are times when brute strength can mean the difference between winning and losing. North Carolina's Mitch Kupchak (left, below) demonstrates this truism as he crunches through two Clemson players who had the temerity to think that they could snatch a loose basketball from his eager grasp. The man who has lost control of the soccer ball at right is Edson Arantes Nascimento—Pelé to you. In 1960, when Pelé was twenty, his native land, Brazil, declared him a national treasure. Fifteen years later he signed a $4.7 million contract to play in the United States—because he generally controls the ball better than anyone alive. Who's on second in the picture below? No, who's on first; what's on second.

The secret of the hula, ladies and gentlemen, is in the hands. In Fig. 1, our Hawaiian demonstrator displays the graceful movement that signifies "Strike one!" Notice the ever so subtle adjustment of the fingers in Fig. 2; they mean "Strike two!" In Fig. 3 we find the classic contortion that is used throughout the islands to signify, "You're out!" And finally, in Fig. 4, its universal antithesis: "Safe!"

RON EDMONDS, HONOLULU STAR-BULLETIN (THIRD PLACE, SPORTS PICTURE STORY)

Togetherness off the field is vital to teamwork on the field. It is important to team morale that squad members travel together, eat together and, er. . . .

Judging the Competition

by Arthur Goldsmith
Editorial Director, Popular Photography

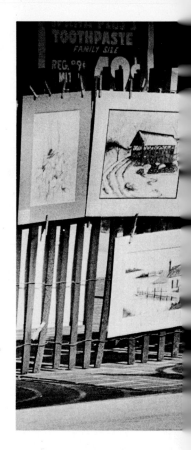

Columbia, Missouri is notable for, among other things, a five-cent cup of coffee (at the airport coffee shop), an eighty-five-cent martini (at the Campus Inn), and the annual Pictures of the Year photojournalism competition (at the University of Missouri). This year's POY, cosponsored by the University of Missouri School of Journalism and the National Press Photographers Association, and funded by an educational grant from Nikon, Inc., was the thirty-fourth since the competition was first started in 1944. Through the ensuing decades POY has established itself as the largest—with almost 10,000 entries this year—and perhaps most important photojournalistic competition in the world.

The tangible rewards can far exceed the cash prizes and plaques handed out during the annual postcompetition awards ceremonies: careers, job opportunities, and professional reputations, especially within the newspaper community, have been strongly influenced by who won what at POY over the years. In addition to the personal impact on those winning an award, the competition has a more general influence: it serves as a model of excellence in photojournalism, a mirror reflecting the best we have in picture-press communication. Award-winning work is studied and emulated by thousands of students and young professionals. Thus, to some degree, each POY is a self-fulfilling prophecy whose entries are conditioned by what kind of pictures won in preceding years. Because of the importance and size of POY, judging it is a singularly demanding task for all those involved in the process.

I have been an observer and critic of the competition for many years, but this was my first on-the-spot experience as a judge, as was the case with all of my fellow judges: Maxwell McCrohon, managing editor of the *Chicago Tribune*; Sean Callahan, photography writer, critic, and editor; George Tames, *New York Times* Washington, D.C. bureau photographer; and Cornelius Keyes, at the time assistant professor of mass communications at Arizona State University. With ages running from thirty-two to fifty-eight, and a wide range of professional backgrounds, we five collectively represented a diversity of viewpoints and experience. We certainly disagreed, sometimes very vehemently, at many points, and I believe all of us had to make some personal compromises to get the job done.

At the end of what had some of the attributes of an intense group encounter session, we not only parted on speaking terms but with the feeling we'd made good new friends. We shared an underlying concern for recognizing excellence and, it seems to me, were generally in agreement on deeper issues if not on details.

The judging experience itself is eyeball-boggling: three solid days of looking and decision-making, starting promptly at 8:30 A.M. and running through, with an hour's lunch break, to as late as 8 P.M. The judging was less of a public event this year than it has been in times past, the *mise en scene* having been shifted from an auditorium to a spartan room in the upper

reaches of the university's huge Hearnes Center. We sat in a row on folding chairs, feeling at first uncomfortably like executioners, with a table in front of us where the pictures were displayed, each of us equipped with an "in"-"out" button box wired into a tabulating device. For the initial screening of each category, the routine was this: Student standing behind big pile of 11 × 14 prints picks one up and hands it to student No. 2. No. 2 holds up the print for the judges to view. Judges push individual "in" or "out" buttons. (Usually, it took two "in" votes to hold at this stage.) Tabulator device goes clickety-click, registering votes, and when all votes are in, it flashes red for "hold" or green for "out." No. 2 passes picture to No. 3 to place in a "hold" or "out" pile, and the next entry immediately is held up for viewing. The pace, with occasional breaks for questions, second looks, and comments, tended to be very fast indeed and developed a certain rhythm. When things were moving, nothing more nor less than

complete concentration was required by all concerned.

Once the initial cut was made, the battle had just begun. The survivors had to be sifted down and ranked first, second, and third in each of some thirty-one different categories. Tabletops were covered and the specially built racks along two sides of the room were filled by mounted prints and tear sheets. Then the analysis, the discussion, the persuasion, the rhetoric, and the argufying commenced. Maybe I'd suggest a picture story I felt strongly about as a possible top winner. Maybe I'd get some support from other judges. Maybe somebody would make a strong pitch for another set. And so it went at that stage, back and forth, until we could hammer out unanimity, or at least a majority. In the process of verbalizing, we also were clarifying to ourselves and the judges just where we really stood with regard to our attitudes toward photography and photojournalism.

We had a lot of conversation, during the judging and during the

gemütlich bull-sessions in the evening, about the "new" photojournalism and trends in picture reporting and what we'd expected to see or hoped to see. I don't think any of us had a clear-cut view of what any of that meant, because it hasn't much happened yet and none of us possesses a crystal ball. What next? Something is stirring, I'm sure, because there has been a recent revolution in newspaper photojournalism. All over the United States, on small-town weeklies and major metropolitan dailies, there is a new generation of press photographers coming. They are mostly college educated, mostly young (and I mean in their early or mid-twenties), both male and female, raised on television and bringing to their jobs a quality of background and visual sophistication that is unprecedented in American newspaper history.

Excerpted from "What's Happening to the Picture Press?" Popular Photography, July 1977. Copyright Ziff-Davis Publishing Co.

Winners

*34th Annual
Pictures of the Year
Competition*

The Nikon World
Understanding Award

NEWSPAPER PHOTOGRAPHER OF THE YEAR

Bruce Bisping, *Minneapolis Tribune*; Runner-up, Jay Mather, Denver Sentinel Newspapers; Third place, Rich Frishman, Pioneer Press, Wilmette, Illinois.

MAGAZINE PHOTOGRAPHER OF THE YEAR

Robert W. Madden, *National Geographic*; Runner-up, James L. Stanfield, *National Geographic*; Third place, Eddie Adams, Associated Press.

WORLD UNDERSTANDING AWARD

Mark and Dan Jury, Waverly, Pennsylvania. Judges' special recognition: Jack Corn, *Nashville Tennessean*; David Cupp, *Denver Post*; and Jim Richardson, *Topeka Capital-Journal*.

NEWSPAPER DIVISION

SPOT NEWS: First, Stanley Forman, *Boston Herald American*, "The Soiling of Old Glory"; Second, Neal Ulevich, Associated Press, "Rightist Strikes Lifeless Body"; Third, George Thompson, *Suburban Trib*, Hinsdale, Illinois, "Get Those Bastards Out of Here." Honorable mention: W. Yates, *Chicago Tribune*, "A Look at Death"; Dean D. Dixon, *Mobile Press Register*, "The Honeymoon's Over"; Bruce M. Fritz, *Capital Times*, Madison, "Scoop Jackson Spitting Incident."

GENERAL NEWS or DOCUMENTARY: First, Don Black, *Binghamton Sun-Bulletin & Press*, "Vice-Presidential Salute"; Second, Ronald S. Karafin, *Passaic Herald News*, "Smoke Gets in His Eyes"; Third, Murry Sill, *Aiken* (S.C.) *Standard*, "That Cute Little Jimmy."

CAMPAIGN '76: First, Nancy Warnecke, *Nashville Tennessean*, "Political Escape"; Second, Lloyd Moebius, *Flint* (Michigan) *Journal*, "Hi There"; Third, Sam Green, *Ottawa* (Kansas) *Herald*, "Peanut Gallery."

FEATURE PICTURE: First, Dave La-Belle, *Goleta* (California) *Today*, "Life Is Full of Obstacles"; Second, Bob Lynn, *Cincinnati Enquirer*, "Bubbled Over"; Third, David Rees, *San Bernardino Sun-Telegram*, "Sitting Down on the Job."

SPORTS ACTION: First, Fraser Hale, *St. Petersburg* (Florida) *Times* and *Evening Independent*, "Pinwheeling at Second"; Second, Ernest Schworck, UPI, "Olympian Yelp"; Third, George Gardner, Jr., *Greenville* (South Carolina) *News*, "One on Two." Honorable mention: Fredric Stein, *Chicago Daily News*, "Ring Around The Runner"; William Meyer, *Milwaukee Journal*, "A Funny Bounce"; Charles Nye, *Eugene Register-Guard* "The Fosbery Flip."

SPORTS FEATURE: First, Rich Frishman, Pioneer Press, Wilmette, Illinois, "Communicating"; Second, Brian Burd, *Lansing State Journal*, "Funeral Before the Competition"; Third, Fred W. Klinger, *Suburban Trib*, Hinsdale, Illinois, "Oh, No." Honorable mention: John Metzger, *San Bernardino Sun-Telegram*, "Mean Billie Jean"; Tom Strongman, Denver Sentinel Newspapers, "Over the Hill Gang."

PORTRAIT/PERSONALITY: First, Jim Wright, *Gainesville Sun*, "Bonita Denny and Kristy"; Second, Flint Born, *Des Moines Register*, "Iva"; Third, Bruce Bisping, *Minneapolis Tribune*, "The Hurt of a Broken Family." Honorable mention: Bob Modersohn, *Des Moines Register*, "Roy 'Snake' White"; Darrell Davidson, *Houston Chronicle*, "Say Cheese."

PICTORIAL: First, Philip Gould, *Dallas Times Herald*, "Group Ballet"; Second, Alan Berner, *Columbia* (Missouri) *Daily Tribune*, "Putting Up the Flag"; Third, Bob Nandell, *Globe-Gazette*, Mason City, Iowa, "Last Recess." Honorable mention: Dale Atkins, *State News*, East Lansing, Michigan,

"Ties to the Past"; Roger Turner, *Wisconsin State Journal*, Madison, "Winter in Dairyland."

EDITORIAL ILLUSTRATION: First, Val Mazzenga, *Chicago Tribune*, "Chicago's Loss"; Second, Brian Burd, *Lansing* (Michigan) *State Journal*, "Tear"; Third, J.G. Domke, *Philadelphia Inquirer*, "Return of the War Toy."

FASHION ILLUSTRATION: First, Jim Klepitsch, *Chicago Sun-Times*, "Urban Male Fashion"; Second, Fredric M. Stein, *Chicago Daily News*, "Beaded Jacket"; Third, J. Ross Baughman, *Lorain* (Ohio) *Journal*, "Feline Finery."

NEWS PICTURE STORY: First, Neal Ulevich, Associated Press, "Bangkok Riots"; Second, Boris Yaro, *Los Angeles Times*, "Plane Crash Fire"; Third, James Parcell, *Washington Post*, "Rescue." Honorable mention: Jay Mather, Denver Sentinel Newspapers, "John Doe to the Other Side"; Bill Wunsch, *Denver Post*, "Clear Creek Rescue"; Charles S. Vallone, *Journal-Times*, Racine, Wisconsin, "Just in Time."

FEATURE PICTURE STORY: First, Rich Frishman, Pioneer Press, Wilmette, Illinois, "Silent Eyes Screaming Songs"; Second, Jay Mather, Denver Sentinel Newspapers, "Carleton Smith's Day at School"; Third, Blair Pittman, *Houston Chronicle*, "Old Railroad Station." Honorable mention: Bruce Bisping, *Minneapolis Tribune*, "The Gandy Dancer."

SPORTS PICTURE STORY: First, Barry Edmonds, *Flint* (Michigan) *Journal*, "Motor Cross Crash"; Second, David Peterson, *Topeka Capital-Journal*, "Big Shot"; Third, Ron Edmonds, *Honolulu Star-Bulletin*, "Hawaiian Ump." Honorable mention: Flint Born, *Des Moines Register*, "West-Side Boxing Club"; Rich Frishman, Pioneer Press, Wilmette, Illinois, "Championship Season."

MAGAZINE DIVISION
CAMPAIGN '76: First, Kit Luce, freelance, "Dole Crying in Gratitude"; Second, Susan T. McElhinney, *Newsweek*, "Barbeque with First Brother Billy"; Third, Dennis Brack, Black Star, "Reagan's Leap."

FEATURE PICTURE: First, Eddie Adams, Associated Press, "New Orleans"; Second, R. W. Madden, *National Geographic*, "Small-Town Sunday"; Third, Kenneth Garrett, *National Geographic*, "New York's Sail Spectacular"; Honorable Mention, James P. Blair, *National Geographic*, "The Lion—South Africa."

SPORTS ACTION: First, Eddie Adams, Associated Press, "Bruce Jenner—Olympic Champion"; Second, Ken Regan, Camera 5, "The Strongest Man in the World"; Third, Mickey Pfleger, freelance, "Winner—Loser."

SPORTS FEATURE: First, Eddie Adams, Associated Press, "Olga Korbut Steps Down for Nadia Comaneci"; Second, James L. Stanfield, *National Geographic*, "Ex-Champions"; Third, E. Adams, Associated Press, "Workout in Lexington."

PORTRAIT/PERSONALITY: First, Jodi Cobb, *National Geographic*, "Buddies"; Second, Martin Rogers, *National Geographic*, "You Deserve a Break Today"; Third, Harry Benson, *People*, "Truman Capote at Home." Honorable mention: David Alan Harvey, *National Geographic*, "Malay Girl"; Dennis Brack, Black Star, "A Moment for Amy."

PICTORIAL: First, Loren McIntyre, *National Geographic*, "Portugal Fishing Boat in Tavira Shoals"; Second, Eddie Adams, Associated Press, "New York, New York"; Third, Eddie Adams, Associated Press, "S.S. *Constellation*." Honorable mention: Bruce Dale, *National Geographic*, "Shore-

birds"; Robert W. Madden, *National Geographic*, "Confluence of Silt River and the Sea."

EDITORIAL ILLUSTRATION: First, Robert W. Madden, *National Geographic*, "Spitting Cobra Strikes."

NEWS or DOCUMENTARY PICTURE STORY: First, James L. Stanfield, *National Geographic*, "Shock Trauma Unit"; Second, James P. Blair, *National Geographic*, "Last Grave at Dimbaza"; Third, James Sugar, *National Geographic*, "Riding the Rails with Hobos."

FEATURE PICTURE STORY: First, James L. Stanfield, *National Geographic*, "Rosier Creek Farm"; Second, Robert W. Madden, *National Geographic*, "Primitive Exorcism of a Malaria Victim"; Third, James L. Stanfield, *National Geographic*, "Our Nation's River —the Potomac"; Honorable mention, Ethan Hoffman, *Columbia Missourian*, "I Divorce You, I Divorce You, I Divorce You."

BEST USE OF PHOTOGRAPHS BY A NEWSPAPER
Claremont (California) *Courier*. Judges' special recognition: *Arlington Heights* (Illinois) *Herald*; *Providence* (Rhode Island) *Journal*.

BEST USE OF PHOTOGRAPHS BY A MAGAZINE
National Geographic.

NEWSPAPER PICTURE EDITOR'S AWARD
Rich Shulman, *Coffeyville* (Kansas) *Journal*. Judges' special recognition: Brian Lanker, *Eugene Register-Guard*; Dick Sroda, *San Bernardino Sun-Telegram*.

MAGAZINE PICTURE EDITOR'S AWARD
Karen Altpeter, *National Wildlife Magazine*.

NEWSPAPER MAGAZINE PICTURE EDITOR'S AWARD
R. Miller, *Des Moines Register*.

Index to Photographers

Robert W. Madden
National Geographic
793-F Fairview Avenue
Annapolis, Maryland 21404
3, 46–49, 61 (right), 212–13

Jay B. Mather
The Courier-Journal
525 West Broadway
Louisville, Kentucky 40202
3, 78–79

Stephanie Maze
The San Francisco Chronicle
Fifth and Mission Streets
San Francisco, California 94119
66

Val Mazzenga
Chicago Tribune
435 N. Michigan Avenue
Chicago, Illinois 60611
21

Chuck McGowen
The News-Journal Company
Wilmington, Delaware 19899
38, 166–69

Wally McNamee
Newsweek
1750 Pennsylvania Ave., N.W.
Washington, D.C. 20006
60

Jim McTaggart
The Minneapolis Star
425 Portland Avenue
Minneapolis, Minnesota 55488
188–89

John Metzger
The Sun-Telegram
San Bernardino, California 92401
228, 250–51

William Meyer
Milwaukee Journal
Journal Square
Milwaukee, Wisconsin 53201
245 (top)

Robert J. Modersohn
Des Moines Register
715 Locust Street
Des Moines, Iowa 50304
77 (bottom)

Lloyd Moebius
Flint Journal
200 East First Street
Flint, Michigan 48502
10 (right)

Earl Morris
5007 Columbia
St. Louis, Missouri 63139
86

Bryan Moss
The Courier-Journal
525 West Broadway
Louisville, Kentucky 40202
28–29, 184–85

Charlie Nye
Sleepy Eye Herald Dispatch
Sleepy Eye, Minnesota 56085
88–89, 94–95, 186–87

Michael O'Brien
The Miami News
One Herald Plaza
Miami, Florida 33132
84–85

James A. Parcell
The Washington Post
1150 15th Street, N.W.
Washington, D.C. 20005
170–71

J.D. Patrick
Wisconsin State Journal
Box 8058
Madison, Wisconsin 53708
11, 238–39

David Peterson
Topeka Capital-Journal
Sixth and Jefferson
Topeka, Kansas 66607
242–43

Blair Pittman
Houston Chronicle
801 Texas
Houston, Texas 77002
214–15

Gene Puskar
Lancaster New Era
8 West King Street
Lancaster, Pennsylvania 17603
39 (bottom)

David Rees
500 So. Garth
Columbia, Missouri 65201
98–99

Larry Reese
Dallas Morning News
Communications Center
Dallas, Texas 75222
16 (below)

Ken Regan
Camera 5
27 W. 27th St.
New York, N.Y.
36, 230, 231(top)

Co Rentmeester
People Magazine
Time Inc.
Time & Life Bldg.
Rockefeller Center

New York, N.Y. 10020
232–33

Donald Roese
Akron Beacon Journal
44 East Exchange Street
Akron, Ohio 44328
97

Jim Richardson
Topeka Capital-Journal
Sixth and Jefferson
Topeka, Kansas 66607
119–33

Greg Schneider
The Sun-Telegram
San Bernardino, California 92401
180–81

Ernest Schworck
United Press International
220 East 42nd Street
New York, N.Y. 10017
231(bottom)

Murry Sill
Aiken Standard
P.O. Box 456
Aiken, South Carolina 29801
16–17, 74

Tony Spina
Detroit Free Press
321 W. Lafayette
Detroit, Michigan 48231
80–81

James L. Stanfield
National Geographic
3606 N. Abingdon
Arlington, Virginia 22207
208–11, 220–23

Christopher Stewart
Watsonville Register-Pajaronian
530 McKenzie Avenue
Watsonville, California 95076
24

Howie Swetz
Westchester-Rockland Newspapers
1 Gannett Drive
White Plains, New York 10604
244 (top)

George Thompson
Suburban Trib
765 North York Road
Hinsdale, Illinois 60521
3

Neal Ulevich
The Associated Press
50 Rockefeller Plaza
New York, N.Y. 10020
54–57

Charles S. Vallone
The Journal-Times

212 Fourth Street
Racine, Wisconsin 53403
178–79

Fred Victorin
St. Petersburg Times and *Evening Independent*
4920 Fourth Avenue So.
St. Petersburg, Florida 33707
86, 87 (bottom)

Suzanne Vlamis
The Associated Press
50 Rockefeller Plaza
New York, N.Y. 10020
63

Fred Ward
Black Star
450 Park Avenue South
New York, N.Y. 10016
1, 61 (left)

Nancy Warnecke
Nashville Tennessean
1100 Broadway
Nashville, Tennessee 37202
75

Larry Williams
St. Louis Post-Dispatch
900 N. 12th Blvd.
St. Louis, Missouri 63101
2

Vic Winter
Kansas State Collegian
109 N. 17th Street
Manhattan, Kansas 66502
12

Michael S. Wirtz
Suburban Trib
765 North York Road
Hinsdale, Illinois 60521
3

Jim Wright
Gainesville Sun
1360 N.E. 32nd Avenue
Gainesville, Florida 32601
90–91

Bill Wunsch
The Denver Post
650 15th Street
Denver, Colorado 80202
176–77

Boris Yaro
Los Angeles Times
202 West First Street
Los Angeles, California 95003
174–75

William Yates
Chicago Tribune
435 North Michigan Avenue
Chicago, Illinois 60611
2

DAVID GRIFFIN, THE POST, OHIO UNIVERSITY